Lighthouse: Beacon of History and Light

MD Shar

Published by pinky, 2024.

While every precaution has been taken in the preparation of this book, the publisher assumes no responsibility for errors or omissions, or for damages resulting from the use of the information contained herein.

LIGHTHOUSE: BEACON OF HISTORY AND LIGHT

First edition. November 6, 2024.

Copyright © 2024 MD Shar.

ISBN: 979-8227286345

Written by MD Shar.

Table of Contents

Preface 1
1. Ala Wai Harbor Lighthouse - USA 5
2. Alcatraz Island Lighthouse - USA 9
3. Alexandria Lighthouse - Egypt 13
4. Arngast Lighthouse - Germany 17
5. Auckland North Head Lighthouse - New Zealand 21
6. Bahía Blanca Lighthouse - Argentina 25
7. Bass Harbor Head Lighthouse - USA 29
8. Bell Rock Lighthouse - UK (Scotland) 33
9. Byron Bay Lighthouse - Australia 37
10. Cabo da Roca Lighthouse - Portugal 41
11. Cabo de São Vicente Lighthouse - Portugal 45
12. Cape Agulhas Lighthouse - South Africa 49
13. Cape Byron Lighthouse - Australia 53
14. Cape Hatteras Lighthouse - USA 57
15. Cape Leeuwin Lighthouse - Australia 61
16. Cape Otway Lighthouse - Australia 65
17. Cape Reinga Lighthouse - New Zealand 69
18. Cape Wrath Lighthouse - UK (Scotland) 73
19. Cordouan Lighthouse - France 77
20. Diamond Head Lighthouse - USA 81
21. Dubh Artach Lighthouse - UK (Scotland) 85
22. Eddystone Lighthouse - UK 89
23. Fanad Head Lighthouse - Ireland 93
24. Faro de Colón - Dominican Republic 97
25. Fastnet Rock Lighthouse - Ireland 101
26. Galle Lighthouse - Sri Lanka 105
27. Gay Head Lighthouse - USA 109
28. Great Basses Reef Lighthouse - Sri Lanka 113
29. Green Point Lighthouse - South Africa 117
30. Heraklion Lighthouse - Greece 121

31. Hook Lighthouse - Ireland 125
32. Jeddah Light - Saudi Arabia 129
33. Kovalam Lighthouse - India 133
34. La Corbière Lighthouse - Jersey (Channel Islands) 137
35. Lindesnes Lighthouse - Norway 141
36. Makapu'u Point Lighthouse - USA 146
37. Malaga Lighthouse - Spain 151
38. Montauk Point Lighthouse - USA 155
39. Peggy's Point Lighthouse - Canada 159
40. Phare des Baleines - France 163
41. Point Reyes Lighthouse - USA 167
42. Portland Head Light - USA 171
43. Punta Carretas Lighthouse - Uruguay 175
44. Ras Gharib Lighthouse - Egypt 179
45. Reykjanesviti Lighthouse - Iceland 183
46. Roter Sand Lighthouse - Germany 187
47. Sambro Island Lighthouse - Canada 192
48. Split Point Lighthouse - Australia 196
49. St. Augustine Lighthouse - USA 200
50. Tower of Hercules - Spain 204
51. Westerheversand Lighthouse – Germany 208

Preface

Lighthouses stand as some of the most enduring symbols of human resilience, innovation, and connection with the sea. Across the world, these beacons have served a purpose far greater than merely guiding ships—they have become guardians of maritime safety, silent witnesses to history, and sources of awe and inspiration for countless generations. This book, Lighthouse: Beacon of History and Light, delves into the fascinating stories of fifty-one of the world's most iconic lighthouses, each one unique in its architecture, history, and cultural significance. From the legendary Tower of Hercules in Spain, with nearly two millennia of history, to the rugged Fastnet Rock in Ireland, each chapter captures the essence of these maritime marvels and the lands they protect.

The idea to write this book emerged from a deep admiration for these structures and their role in our shared history. While most of us may never stand as lighthouse keepers or navigate treacherous waters, lighthouses remain powerful symbols in our collective imagination. They evoke a sense of adventure, solitude, and steadfastness. In a world where digital technology has reshaped navigation, these physical towers continue to mark our coastlines, embodying the resilience of both the past and the people who maintain them.

Lighthouses have a long and rich history that reaches back thousands of years. The earliest known lighthouse was the famed Pharos of Alexandria, built around 280 BCE by the Ptolemaic Kingdom of Ancient Egypt. Standing over 100 meters tall, the Pharos was considered one of the Seven Wonders of the Ancient World, guiding ships into the busy harbor of Alexandria for centuries before it was eventually destroyed by earthquakes. This magnificent structure set the stage for the construction of other lighthouses, as civilizations recognized the critical need for navigational aids along hazardous coastlines. The Tower of Hercules, built by the Romans on the Spanish coast, is the oldest operational lighthouse in the world, dating back nearly 2,000 years. Its continuous use is a testament to both its construction and the strategic location it commands.

Throughout history, lighthouses have played an invaluable role in maritime travel. Before advanced navigational tools like radar, GPS, or sonar, sailors relied heavily on visual cues to avoid dangerous rocks, reefs, and shorelines, particularly at night or during foggy weather. A lighthouse's powerful beam, often visible for miles, served as a vital guide, warning mariners of impending danger and providing them with bearings to navigate safely to their destination. Lighthouses also served as landmarks, each with its distinct flash pattern, helping sailors determine their exact location along the coast.

Today, thousands of lighthouses dot the shores of oceans, rivers, and lakes worldwide. While many are automated, and some have even been retired from their original function, lighthouses continue to be significant, standing as reminders of the past and serving as both navigational aids and cultural treasures. Each lighthouse has a story, not just of its construction, but of the countless lives it has protected and the community that grew around it. This book aims to bring these stories to life, presenting a blend of architectural beauty, historical depth, and cultural resonance.

In Lighthouse: Beacon of History and Light, readers will find stories that span centuries and continents. Each chapter introduces a new lighthouse and transports the reader to a different part of the world, from the windswept shores of Scotland to the tropical coasts of the Dominican Republic. This journey through lighthouses highlights how varied and widespread these structures are, reflecting the diverse ways in which different cultures and civilizations have approached the challenge of maritime safety.

The reader will discover the early challenges of building lighthouses in difficult and remote locations, from rugged cliffs to isolated islands. In many cases, the construction of these towers tested the limits of

LIGHTHOUSE: BEACON OF HISTORY AND LIGHT

contemporary engineering, resulting in architectural innovations that have inspired generations. The story of the Eddystone Lighthouse in the UK, for example, is one of trial and error, with multiple versions of the structure constructed over time due to the extreme challenges posed by its exposed location. The Fastnet Rock Lighthouse in Ireland, perched on a small, storm-battered islet, is another example of how human determination triumphed over adversity.

This book is also an exploration of the lives of those who maintained these lighthouses, often in isolation and under challenging conditions. Many lighthouse keepers and their families lived in remote locations, experiencing both solitude and a unique sense of responsibility. The lives of these keepers—people who maintained the lights long before automation—are intertwined with the history of these structures. Their dedication ensured that the lights continued to shine, even through the darkest nights and most turbulent storms. These stories of resilience add depth to each lighthouse's history, reminding us that lighthouses are more than just structures; they are part of the human journey.

But the purpose of this book is not solely historical. It is also an invitation to view these lighthouses as symbols that resonate in today's world. Lighthouses represent a steady, guiding light, something we all seek in moments of uncertainty. They offer a quiet strength, standing tall despite the ravages of time and nature, reminding us of endurance, guidance, and hope. For anyone who has ever felt inspired by a lighthouse, this book offers a chance to understand these beacons on a deeper level, to learn about the history that shaped them and the legacies they carry.

As we journey through these tales of light and history, we hope readers will feel a renewed connection to the sea, to history, and the resilience of human endeavor. In an age when technology has transformed navigation, lighthouses remain steadfast, bridging the past and the present. They continue to mark coastlines and shores, sometimes as functional aids, other times as historic monuments, and always as silent witnesses to humanity's relationship with the sea.

Lighthouse: Beacon of History and Light is for everyone who is drawn to the sea, and who finds inspiration in the persistence of structures that have withstood centuries of storms and solitude. This book celebrates the lighthouses of the world not only as architectural feats but as cultural touchstones, markers of history, and symbols of resilience. In these pages, readers will encounter lighthouses that have protected lives, witnessed history, and become beloved landmarks. Whether you are an enthusiast of maritime history, a lover of architecture, or simply curious about these beacons of light, this book offers a journey worth taking. Step inside and let the stories of these lighthouses illuminate the path through the captivating world of maritime history.

—**Author**

1. Ala Wai Harbor Lighthouse - USA

The Ala Wai Harbor Lighthouse stands quietly on the shores of Honolulu, Hawaii, casting its light into the azure expanse of the Pacific Ocean. Small and modest in size compared to grander lighthouses, it remains an essential guidepost, directing seafarers away from danger and welcoming them to the bustling harbor. The structure, a white tower topped with a hint of red, rises with a simplicity that resonates with the island's tranquil spirit. Although not tall or imposing, the lighthouse has a sturdy charm, making it a beloved sight among the yachts and small boats that pass by daily.

Built during the early years of Hawaii's modernization, the Ala Wai Harbor Lighthouse's history is woven into Honolulu's transformation. It was established when the harbor began its development as a recreational and economic center, which brought in more maritime traffic. This beacon provided a crucial guiding light, ensuring the safe navigation of vessels into the relatively narrow, bustling channel. As a part of Hawaii's growing infrastructural landscape, the lighthouse was instrumental in promoting maritime safety and supporting the burgeoning local economy.

Honolulu, where the Ala Wai Harbor Lighthouse is located, enjoys a tropical climate. Temperatures remain warm throughout the year, generally ranging between 75°F to 85°F. Trade winds blowing across the islands provide a refreshing coolness, and the area experiences a mix of sun-drenched days and intermittent tropical rain showers. This climate contributes to the lush surroundings of the lighthouse, where palm trees sway gently in the breeze, and vibrant native plants like hibiscus and plumeria thrive.

The Ala Wai Harbor Lighthouse isn't just a practical structure; it's an iconic symbol. Its light has safely guided countless recreational and fishing boats, contributing significantly to the harbor's reputation as a world-class boating destination. Its surroundings are teeming with tropical flora that attracts birds and small animals, lending a natural harmony to this otherwise busy harbor. The waters are frequented by native marine life, from schools of colorful fish to graceful sea turtles that glide through the clear waves nearby. Occasionally, one might even spot dolphins playing in the distance, adding a sense of enchantment to the atmosphere.

Despite its significance, the Ala Wai Harbor Lighthouse remains relatively low-profile, which only adds to its charm. It is a hidden gem known primarily to locals and seasoned mariners. Its existence has subtly influenced Honolulu's social landscape, fostering a community of maritime enthusiasts and nature lovers who frequent the harbor. Many locals and visitors alike hold the lighthouse in fond regard, associating it with the serene beauty of the harbor, as well as with memories of sunny days spent on the water.

The lighthouse has witnessed Honolulu's transformation over the years, adapting to the challenges that come with increased tourism and urban development. The harbor area is a hub of activity, often bustling with visitors, particularly during the high tourist season. As such, the lighthouse and its surrounding areas face the usual urban challenges, including the need for regular maintenance, protection of the local

LIGHTHOUSE: BEACON OF HISTORY AND LIGHT

ecosystem, and preservation efforts against erosion and pollution. Maintaining this small but mighty lighthouse is essential to retaining Honolulu's cultural and historical landscape.

Few people know that the Ala Wai Harbor Lighthouse is also a part of Hawaii's network of navigational aids, which stretch across the islands to guide sailors safely around Hawaii's diverse and sometimes treacherous coastlines. Its light, though modest, is a part of this larger system, connecting it to a legacy of exploration and maritime tradition. Interestingly, because of its size and location, the lighthouse isn't usually open to the public, and only a small number of people have had the opportunity to see it up close. This exclusivity lends an air of mystery to the lighthouse, enhancing its appeal.

The lighthouse's importance goes beyond its function as a navigational aid. For Honolulu's residents, it serves as a reminder of the city's rich maritime history, symbolizing resilience and connection to the vast ocean that surrounds Hawaii. As such, it has become an enduring symbol, embodying the island spirit of warmth, welcome, and adventure. Its steady light is a comforting sight, an unassuming beacon that promises safe passage to those who sail by.

The Ala Wai Harbor is well-connected by various transport options, making it accessible to travelers from all around the world. Honolulu International Airport lies just a short drive away, and from there, a combination of buses, taxis, and ride-sharing services makes it easy for visitors to reach the harbor. Tourists can rent bicycles or walk along the waterfront paths, catching glimpses of the lighthouse and its surroundings. The harbor also offers mooring facilities for private boats and yachts, attracting a mix of locals and international travelers eager to explore Hawaii by sea.

As dusk falls and the sky fades to shades of purple and orange, the Ala Wai Harbor Lighthouse quietly takes center stage. Its light flickers on, casting a gentle glow across the water, signaling to sailors as it has done for decades. The lighthouse may not be the tallest or the grandest, but it remains a beloved landmark, a steadfast presence on Honolulu's vibrant shores. Its story, much like its light, is one of quiet strength and understated beauty, an enduring part of Hawaii's coastal charm.

2. Alcatraz Island Lighthouse - USA

The Alcatraz Island Lighthouse stands as a silent guardian on a rugged, rocky outcrop in the middle of San Francisco Bay. The lighthouse, a tall, whitewashed structure with a worn appearance, rises above the cliffs of Alcatraz Island, known more famously for its notorious federal prison. This lighthouse has witnessed the fog-shrouded mysteries and the harsh gales that sweep through the bay, its beam a lifeline for sailors navigating these often turbulent waters.

Built in 1854, Alcatraz Island Lighthouse was the first lighthouse on the West Coast, marking an important step in the development of maritime infrastructure in the region. The original structure, however, was replaced in 1909 with the current tower, designed to withstand the challenging coastal weather. Over the years, the lighthouse has evolved, but it has never wavered in its commitment to lighting the way for vessels traveling into the Bay Area.

Situated in San Francisco Bay, Alcatraz Island experiences a temperate Mediterranean climate, with mild, damp winters and dry summers. Temperatures remain relatively consistent, ranging between 50°F and 65°F. The frequent fog that drifts across the bay lends the area a mystique, enhancing the island's atmosphere. The lighthouse, with its rotating beam, was critical in helping mariners avoid the dangerous cliffs and rocks surrounding Alcatraz, especially in the fog's dense shroud.

The Alcatraz Island Lighthouse holds historical significance as a guiding light for ships entering San Francisco Bay, one of the busiest ports on the West Coast. While its role as a navigational aid is now less crucial due to modern technology, the lighthouse remains a cultural icon and a powerful symbol of maritime heritage. It is part of the island's National Historic Landmark status, drawing visitors fascinated by its unique blend of history and mystery.

Alcatraz Island is not only known for its lighthouse and prison but also for its rich ecosystem. Sparse vegetation dots the island, mainly composed of hardy, salt-resistant plants that can survive the rocky, windswept environment. The island is home to a variety of bird species, particularly seabirds like gulls, cormorants, and pelicans. These birds, nesting among the cliffs, add life and sound to the otherwise eerie landscape. Occasionally, seals and sea lions can be seen basking on the nearby rocks, their calls echoing across the bay. Despite its isolation and harsh environment, Alcatraz supports a small but vibrant ecological community.

The lighthouse's social impact extends beyond its practical use. As a symbol, it has played a role in shaping perceptions of Alcatraz. While the prison may evoke feelings of confinement and desolation, the lighthouse serves as a beacon of hope, shining brightly even in the darkest hours. For those incarcerated on the island, the lighthouse was perhaps a symbol of the world beyond, a world that continued to exist despite the prison walls. Today, it stands as a reminder of the island's layered history, blending narratives of hope and hardship.

Alcatraz Island and its lighthouse face numerous challenges, particularly related to preservation. The salty sea air, strong winds, and regular fog have taken their toll on the structure. Maintaining the

LIGHTHOUSE: BEACON OF HISTORY AND LIGHT

lighthouse and other historic buildings on Alcatraz requires ongoing restoration efforts. The island is managed by the National Park Service, which works diligently to preserve its history while accommodating the many tourists who visit annually.

The Alcatraz Lighthouse has its own share of lesser-known facts. For instance, the island was named "La Isla de los Alcatraces" (Island of the Pelicans) by Spanish explorer Juan Manuel de Ayala, a name inspired by the abundance of seabirds on the island. Few people realize that the lighthouse served as a communication link as well, with the lighthouse keepers signaling ships before the installation of modern radio technology. In the 1960s, Alcatraz Lighthouse became fully automated, a transition that marked the end of an era when keepers personally tended the light.

The lighthouse's importance goes beyond guiding ships; it is a piece of California's history, symbolizing the state's emergence as a major maritime hub. The light it casts has guided countless ships safely to shore, allowing San Francisco to thrive as a commercial center. Over the years, it has served as a point of reference for those navigating not only the physical waters of the bay but also the cultural tides that define this region. Alcatraz Island Lighthouse is a beacon that connects past to present, a tangible reminder of San Francisco's role in the development of the Western United States.

Reaching Alcatraz Island is an adventure in itself. Ferries operate regularly from San Francisco's Pier 33, bringing visitors from around the world to explore the infamous prison and the historic lighthouse. The journey offers spectacular views of the Golden Gate Bridge and the San Francisco skyline, creating an experience that blends natural beauty with historical exploration. While the lighthouse no longer plays an essential role in navigation, it remains a point of interest for history enthusiasts, photographers, and curious travelers alike.

As the sun sets over San Francisco Bay, the Alcatraz Island Lighthouse casts its light across the water, a silent observer of the shifting tides and the city's ever-evolving story. Standing steadfast through decades of change, it endures as a symbol of resilience, a testament to the passage of time and the enduring importance of safe passage for all those who venture into the bay.

3. Alexandria Lighthouse - Egypt

The Lighthouse of Alexandria, known as the Pharos of Alexandria, once stood as a marvel of the ancient world, guiding sailors into the bustling port city of Alexandria, Egypt. Constructed on the small island of Pharos in the 3rd century BCE, this towering structure reached approximately 100 meters, making it one of the tallest man-made structures of its time. The Pharos, with its three-tiered design—a square base, an octagonal middle section, and a cylindrical top—was a testament to the architectural prowess of the ancient Egyptians and Greeks, merging function with a grandeur that would captivate the ancient world.

Built during the reign of Ptolemy II, the lighthouse was conceived as a response to Alexandria's growing importance as a trade center. The city, founded by Alexander the Great, quickly became a hub of commerce and knowledge, attracting traders, philosophers, and scholars from across the known world. With this increased maritime traffic, the need for a beacon to safely guide ships into the city's harbor became paramount. The Pharos was designed by the Greek architect Sostratus of Cnidus, and it served not only as a guiding light but also as a symbol of Alexandria's wealth and ambition.

The lighthouse's location on Pharos Island was strategically chosen for its proximity to the city and the visibility it offered across the Mediterranean. Alexandria itself experiences a hot desert climate, though the Mediterranean Sea moderates temperatures along the coast. Summers are warm and dry, with temperatures often rising above 86°F (30°C), while winters are mild, usually ranging between 50°F and 68°F (10-20°C). The Pharos was visible day and night, and in the warmer months, its guiding light became especially valuable as the skies grew hazy with the heat.

As a beacon, the Pharos of Alexandria was invaluable to sailors. Its light, powered by a fire that burned continuously at its peak, could be seen from miles away. Reflective mirrors amplified the light, allowing it to reach even further out to sea. The lighthouse helped countless ships avoid the dangerous coastline, guiding them safely into the busy harbor of Alexandria. It wasn't only a navigational aid but also a welcome sight for weary sailors, symbolizing the safety of land and the vibrant life of Alexandria's port.

While Alexandria was known more for its bustling streets and grand library, Pharos Island was a quieter area, characterized by its rocky terrain and sparse vegetation. The plants that did grow here were hardy, able to survive the island's saline soil and occasional sea spray. Seabirds often flocked to the island, nesting on the cliffs around the lighthouse and feeding on fish from the nearby waters. These birds added life to the island's rocky shores, contrasting with the otherwise stark landscape of the lighthouse.

The Pharos had a profound social impact, becoming a cultural symbol of Alexandria's status as a world city. It featured on coins, in literature, and in the stories of travelers who marveled at its imposing structure. Beyond its practical use, it served as a point of pride for Alexandrians, embodying their city's sophistication and reach. For centuries, the

LIGHTHOUSE: BEACON OF HISTORY AND LIGHT

lighthouse stood as a symbol of human ingenuity and the quest for knowledge, which was also reflected in Alexandria's famed library and its reputation as a center of learning.

However, the Pharos faced many challenges over the centuries. Built on an island, it was exposed to the full force of the Mediterranean's elements, including powerful storms and the occasional earthquake. These natural forces eventually took their toll. Although the lighthouse stood strong for centuries, several earthquakes struck the region between the 10th and 14th centuries, each one weakening its structure further. By the 14th century, it had collapsed, leaving only remnants of what was once a symbol of Alexandria's greatness.

One of the lesser-known facts about the Pharos is that it was considered one of the Seven Wonders of the Ancient World, a title that placed it alongside structures like the Great Pyramid of Giza and the Hanging Gardens of Babylon. While most people are familiar with the lighthouse's function as a navigational aid, few realize it was also used as an observation post, with a large statue of Zeus or Poseidon (depending on the account) at its summit. This statue gazed out over the Mediterranean, a silent guardian of Alexandria.

The Pharos was important not only for its role in navigation but also for its significance as an engineering masterpiece. It was one of the first structures to use limestone and marble, materials that enhanced its visibility in daylight and gave it a luminous quality at dusk. Its mirror system, which reflected the light of the fire, was an advanced technological feature for the time, allowing the light to reach distances previously thought impossible.

During its centuries of operation, the lighthouse saw visitors from across the Mediterranean and beyond. Traders, explorers, and scholars arrived in Alexandria by boat, drawn to its reputation for knowledge and wealth. Today, the ruins of the Pharos serve as a reminder of these ancient connections. The site is accessible by ferry from Alexandria's mainland, and although the lighthouse itself is no longer standing, the journey to Pharos Island remains a pilgrimage of sorts for those drawn to the legend of this ancient wonder.

As evening descended on ancient Alexandria, the Pharos would light up, its fire a beacon in the growing darkness. For those at sea, it was a welcome sight, a promise of safe harbor after long and perilous journeys. While it has now passed into history, the Pharos of Alexandria remains alive in the stories, artworks, and symbols it has inspired across generations. Standing tall even in ruins, it continues to symbolize a city that once led the world in knowledge and ambition.

4. Arngast Lighthouse - Germany

The Arngast Lighthouse, rising tall and solitary in the Wadden Sea off Germany's northern coast, is an emblem of resilience and maritime history. Built in the early 20th century, this red-and-white striped lighthouse is situated on a small sandbank in the Jade Bight, a bay in the North Sea. Standing approximately 36 meters tall, the lighthouse appears almost isolated in the vast expanse of shallow water and tidal flats that characterize this unique environment. The Wadden Sea, known for its extensive mudflats and intertidal ecosystems, creates a landscape that shifts dramatically with the tides, rendering the lighthouse accessible by boat only at high tide.

Arngast Lighthouse was constructed in 1910 to address the growing maritime needs of the Wilhelmshaven port, a major naval and commercial harbor in Germany. Positioned strategically, the lighthouse guides vessels safely through the narrow and shifting channels of the Jade Bight. Before the construction of the Arngast Lighthouse, navigation in these waters was challenging due to the region's sandbanks and frequently changing tidal patterns. The lighthouse's powerful beacon and distinctive shape provided a critical navigational aid, helping countless ships avoid running aground and safely find their way into the port.

The climate around the Arngast Lighthouse is marked by cold winters and mild, breezy summers. Temperatures range from around 30°F in the winter to about 70°F in the warmer months. The area experiences frequent winds sweeping across the North Sea, and thick fog often envelops the lighthouse, reducing visibility for both sailors and visitors. These conditions underscore the importance of the lighthouse's light, which can pierce through even the densest fog, providing a reliable beacon in otherwise disorienting weather.

Arngast Lighthouse remains a popular landmark, admired for its isolation and stark beauty. Its usefulness as a navigational aid endures, though modern technology has supplemented its role. Today, the lighthouse serves as a cherished reminder of the region's maritime heritage, attracting visitors who journey by boat to view its striking silhouette against the sky. The lighthouse's isolated position on a sandbank also means that it is surrounded by unique flora and fauna, with patches of seaweed and hardy salt-tolerant plants thriving around its base. The Wadden Sea is teeming with life, home to numerous bird species like gulls, sandpipers, and plovers, which find ample food in the mudflats exposed at low tide. Seals are frequently spotted lounging on nearby sandbanks, basking in the sun, or watching curiously as boats pass.

Socially, the lighthouse has become an icon for the coastal communities around Wilhelmshaven and the surrounding areas. It represents a connection to the sea, embodying the tenacity and skill of generations of sailors and lighthouse keepers who braved the harsh elements to ensure the safety of those navigating the waters. For locals, the lighthouse is a symbol of endurance against the ever-changing forces of nature, and it holds a cherished place in the hearts of those who live by the sea.

LIGHTHOUSE: BEACON OF HISTORY AND LIGHT

Located far from the mainland, the Arngast Lighthouse faces numerous challenges. The Wadden Sea's dynamic environment exposes the structure to constant weathering from wind, water, and shifting sands. The maintenance of the lighthouse is difficult, given its remote location and the need for specialized equipment to access it during specific tidal conditions. Despite these challenges, efforts to preserve the lighthouse continue, ensuring that it remains a part of the region's maritime landscape.

One lesser-known fact about the Arngast Lighthouse is its role in the local ecosystem. As a relatively isolated structure, it has become a resting point for migratory birds. Its light, especially at dusk and dawn, attracts certain marine species, adding a subtle but fascinating layer to the biodiversity of the Wadden Sea. The surrounding mudflats, designated a UNESCO World Heritage site, are themselves part of a fragile ecosystem, making the lighthouse a rare human structure in an otherwise untouched environment.

The importance of the Arngast Lighthouse goes beyond its immediate function as a guiding light. Historically, it facilitated safe passage into Wilhelmshaven, a port that played a significant role in both commerce and naval operations. Even today, as ships from around the world pass by on their way into German waters, the lighthouse serves as a reassuring presence, a beacon in the vast and often challenging North Sea. It stands as a testament to the ingenuity and dedication of those who built it, as well as to the importance of maritime infrastructure in supporting global trade.

Reaching the Arngast Lighthouse requires careful planning, as it is accessible only by boat, with tours organized for visitors eager to explore this piece of maritime history. These journeys provide a unique experience, taking travelers across the Wadden Sea and offering views of the tidal flats, sandbanks, and the serene beauty of the coastline. For those visiting the area, the lighthouse is a fascinating destination, a place where the isolation and beauty of the sea come together with the rich history of Germany's coastal heritage.

As the tides ebb and flow, the Arngast Lighthouse stands resilient, its light shining steadily across the waters. It is more than a navigational aid; it is a symbol of the enduring connection between humanity and the sea, a silent guardian watching over the ever-shifting landscape of the Wadden Sea.

5. Auckland North Head Lighthouse - New Zealand

The Auckland North Head Lighthouse sits gracefully on the hill at North Head, overlooking the vibrant waters of Waitematā Harbour in Auckland, New Zealand. The modest structure, painted white with a red-topped lantern room, is not particularly tall, but its location gives it a commanding view of the harbor, the city skyline, and the Hauraki Gulf. This lighthouse, though unassuming in size, has served as a crucial navigational aid for ships approaching Auckland since it was established in the late 19th century.

Constructed in 1893, the Auckland North Head Lighthouse was built as part of Auckland's response to the increasing maritime traffic in its harbor. The city was growing quickly, driven by trade and the influx of settlers, and North Head was already a strategic point, having served as a military outpost for years. The lighthouse's location on North Head was ideal, giving it a sweeping view of incoming vessels and allowing its light to be seen by ships navigating the often challenging waters of the harbor.

Auckland enjoys a mild maritime climate, with warm, humid summers and mild, damp winters. Temperatures typically range from 59°F to 77°F (15°C to 25°C) in the summer and 46°F to 59°F (8°C to 15°C) in the winter. This temperate climate contributes to the lush greenery surrounding the lighthouse, where native plants like pohutukawa trees flourish. These trees, also known as New Zealand Christmas trees, produce brilliant red flowers in summer, adding a vibrant touch to the landscape around the lighthouse.

The Auckland North Head Lighthouse has become an iconic symbol for sailors and locals alike. Though its primary function has been supplanted by modern navigation technologies, the lighthouse remains a comforting sight for those entering the harbor. It also attracts numerous visitors who come to explore North Head's historical sites and take in the panoramic views. The lighthouse stands as a reminder of Auckland's maritime history, representing the city's growth and its connection to the sea.

The flora around North Head is rich with native New Zealand vegetation, including coastal shrubs and ferns that thrive in the salty air. Pohutukawa trees, known for their resilience and beauty, dominate the landscape and provide shade and shelter for a variety of birds. The lighthouse grounds are frequented by seabirds like gannets and terns, which nest along the coast. In the surrounding waters, dolphins and orcas are occasional visitors, adding to the sense of wonder that surrounds this peaceful site.

For Auckland's residents, the lighthouse at North Head holds a special place in local culture. It has become more than a navigational aid; it is a landmark of the city's identity and a symbol of its seafaring past. The lighthouse, together with the old military bunkers on North Head, gives visitors a glimpse into Auckland's historical layers. The area has been a favorite spot for families, picnickers, and history enthusiasts who come to explore the scenic hill and its historic structures.

LIGHTHOUSE: BEACON OF HISTORY AND LIGHT

The location of the Auckland North Head Lighthouse presents a few challenges. The hilltop where it stands is exposed to strong coastal winds, and the salty air can be harsh on the structure, necessitating regular maintenance. Efforts to preserve the lighthouse and the surrounding historic sites are ongoing, ensuring that this piece of Auckland's heritage remains intact for future generations.

A lesser-known fact about the Auckland North Head Lighthouse is its role during the World Wars. North Head was fortified with gun emplacements and bunkers, which were intended to protect the harbor from potential attacks. While the lighthouse itself was not part of the defense systems, its presence at this strategic point meant it remained a symbol of both guidance and vigilance. Today, visitors can still explore these bunkers and enjoy the sweeping views of the harbor, with the lighthouse as a quiet but steadfast companion.

The lighthouse holds great importance as a beacon of Auckland's maritime legacy. Positioned at the entrance to one of New Zealand's busiest ports, it has witnessed countless ships passing by, from early wooden vessels to modern cargo ships. Its light once guided them safely to shore, symbolizing the city's hospitality and its role as a gateway to New Zealand. Even though it no longer serves as a primary navigational aid, the lighthouse remains an enduring symbol of Auckland's connection to the sea.

Getting to the Auckland North Head Lighthouse is relatively easy, with various transportation options available. The ferry from downtown Auckland to Devonport provides a scenic route, and from Devonport, a short walk or drive takes visitors to North Head. The area is well-serviced by local buses, and for those exploring the city on foot, the route to North Head offers views of Auckland's harbor, parks, and neighborhoods.

As evening falls over Waitematā Harbour, the Auckland North Head Lighthouse stands quietly against the sky, a symbol of Auckland's past and present. It is a place where history and nature meet, where the beauty of the land blends seamlessly with the stories of those who once relied on its light. Standing at the edge of New Zealand's largest city, it is a reminder of the enduring connection between the people of Auckland and the vast ocean that shapes their lives.

6. Bahía Blanca Lighthouse - Argentina

The Bahía Blanca Lighthouse, standing tall along the rugged coast of Argentina, is a powerful symbol of guidance and resilience. Located in the Buenos Aires Province, near the bustling port city of Bahía Blanca, this lighthouse has been an essential part of Argentina's maritime history for more than a century. Painted in striking black and white stripes, it stands out against the coastline, serving as a beacon for ships navigating the South Atlantic. Its height, though not towering compared to some modern lighthouses, gives it a sturdy and unyielding presence on the edge of the continent, a fitting emblem of strength against the ocean's force.

Established in the early 20th century, the Bahía Blanca Lighthouse was part of a strategic development to support Argentina's growing maritime activities. Bahía Blanca itself was becoming an important trade center, with its port facilitating the transportation of agricultural goods and other exports. The lighthouse was built to help ships safely navigate the often-turbulent waters and avoid the rocky coastline. Its light, visible for miles, has guided countless vessels into the safety of the port, making it a vital part of Argentina's infrastructure.

Located on the eastern coast of South America, Bahía Blanca experiences a semi-arid climate with a mix of humid and dry seasons. Temperatures vary significantly, with hot, dry summers where the mercury can rise above 95°F (35°C) and cooler winters, dropping to an average of around 45°F (7°C). Winds from the ocean are common, and the lighthouse's location subjects it to the full brunt of these coastal breezes, which add to the lighthouse's rugged character. The sea's salty air contributes to the weathering of the lighthouse's exterior, necessitating regular maintenance to keep it functioning and looking its best.

The lighthouse's distinctive black and white stripes have made it a recognizable landmark, not only for mariners but also for locals and tourists. Over the years, it has become a beloved symbol of the Bahía Blanca community. Although its role in navigation has been somewhat reduced by modern technology, the lighthouse remains a reassuring sight for sailors and a popular destination for visitors who appreciate its historical significance. The view from the lighthouse offers sweeping vistas of the Atlantic and the windswept coastline, making it a picturesque spot for photographers and nature enthusiasts.

The flora around Bahía Blanca Lighthouse consists mainly of coastal grasses, hardy shrubs, and small patches of wildflowers that bloom in the warmer months. The vegetation is sparse, adapted to the dry, sandy soil and the coastal winds. Despite the harsh environment, a variety of wildlife can be found here, including seabirds such as gulls and cormorants that nest along the cliffs. The rocky shores below the lighthouse are sometimes visited by sea lions, which bask in the sun or swim near the shoreline, creating a lively natural setting that enhances the charm of the lighthouse.

For the people of Bahía Blanca and nearby communities, the lighthouse is more than a navigational aid. It is a cultural icon, a reminder of Argentina's maritime heritage and its ties to the Atlantic. The lighthouse has witnessed the evolution of the port and the

LIGHTHOUSE: BEACON OF HISTORY AND LIGHT

surrounding city, reflecting the growth of Argentina's economy and its connection to the rest of the world. Generations of locals have visited the lighthouse, taking pride in its history and resilience, and it has become a symbol of continuity amid change.

However, the Bahía Blanca Lighthouse faces numerous challenges. The constant exposure to the elements, especially the salty sea air and strong winds, accelerates the wear and tear on the structure. Regular maintenance is essential to preserve its functionality and appearance, and while the Argentine government has invested in its upkeep, the lighthouse requires ongoing care to stand firm against the Atlantic's relentless forces. The remote location also means that repairs and inspections are logistically challenging, adding to the difficulty of preserving this historical landmark.

One interesting fact about the Bahía Blanca Lighthouse is its role in the local shipping industry. In its early years, it was a crucial point of reference for sailors, who relied on its light to guide them into the port. Additionally, the lighthouse is strategically positioned along a route that connects Argentina to major international shipping lanes, making it an essential landmark not only for local vessels but for international cargo ships as well. Its beam of light has been a welcome sight for ships traveling to and from various parts of the world, linking Bahía Blanca with distant shores.

The lighthouse holds significant importance beyond its practical function. It has stood as a silent witness to Argentina's history, from the early days of the country's trade expansion to modern times. It has been there through changes in the economy, shifts in political landscapes, and advances in technology. Its light has continued to shine, a steady presence on the coast, embodying Argentina's enduring connection to the sea and the rest of the world. For sailors, it represents safety; for locals, it is a treasured piece of heritage; and for travelers, it is a fascinating landmark that offers a glimpse into Argentina's maritime culture.

Access to the Bahía Blanca Lighthouse is limited, given its isolated location on the coast. However, local boat tours often pass by the lighthouse, allowing visitors to view it from the water. The nearest major transport hub is the Bahía Blanca port, where ships from across the globe dock. For those on land, a short drive from Bahía Blanca takes visitors to a viewpoint overlooking the lighthouse and the coastline, providing an opportunity to see this iconic structure up close and enjoy the scenic landscape.

As the sun sets over the Atlantic and the sky fills with hues of pink and orange, the Bahía Blanca Lighthouse continues its watch, casting a steady light across the water. It is a symbol of guidance and endurance, a reminder of the strength required to stand firm against the challenges of the ocean. For all who see it, the lighthouse is a source of inspiration, a link between past and present, and a testament to Argentina's spirit. Standing at the edge of the continent, it embodies the courage and resilience of those who live by the sea, their lives shaped by the constant ebb and flow of the tides.

7. Bass Harbor Head Lighthouse - USA

Bass Harbor Head Lighthouse stands on the rugged coast of Mount Desert Island in Maine, a striking sentinel overlooking the vast Atlantic Ocean. Perched on a rocky cliff at the entrance to Bass Harbor, this small but iconic lighthouse has guided mariners safely through these waters for over a century. Built in 1858, the lighthouse is a charming white structure topped with a red lantern room, and while it may not be one of the tallest lighthouses, its location on the cliffside elevates it, giving it a majestic view of the ocean and coastline.

The history of Bass Harbor Head Lighthouse is closely tied to Maine's rich maritime tradition. Established to help manage the growing maritime traffic around Mount Desert Island, the lighthouse was crucial in aiding the fishing and shipping industries that relied on safe passage through the sometimes treacherous coastal waters. Its beam warned ships off the rocks below and helped them navigate around the island toward safe harbors. Built with a sturdy design, the lighthouse was constructed to withstand Maine's challenging coastal weather and has been well-preserved over the years.

Located within Acadia National Park, Bass Harbor Head Lighthouse benefits from Maine's distinctive coastal climate. Summers are mild and pleasant, with temperatures averaging between 60°F and 75°F (15°C to 24°C), and winters are cold, often dipping below freezing. The lighthouse is frequently exposed to powerful Atlantic storms, which bring high winds and heavy rain. These seasonal changes bring a different character to the lighthouse, from misty, atmospheric mornings in autumn to bright, clear days in summer. In all seasons, the landscape around the lighthouse transforms, showcasing Maine's natural beauty.

Over time, the Bass Harbor Head Lighthouse has become one of the most photographed lighthouses in the United States. Its striking location on a rocky promontory, framed by dense evergreen trees and dramatic cliffs, makes it a picturesque destination for photographers and tourists alike. While it continues to serve as an active navigational aid, its popularity has grown due to its scenic beauty, making it a significant attraction within Acadia National Park. Visitors flock to the area to enjoy the breathtaking views and witness the sunset casting a warm glow over the lighthouse and the Atlantic.

The flora surrounding Bass Harbor Head Lighthouse is typical of Maine's coastal ecosystem, with hardy trees like spruces and firs lining the path to the lighthouse. Coastal shrubs and wildflowers add color to the landscape during spring and summer. The area is also rich in wildlife; seabirds like gulls and cormorants nest along the rocky cliffs, and eagles are often seen soaring above the coastline. The waters around the lighthouse are home to diverse marine life, including seals that can be spotted basking on the rocks and dolphins occasionally appearing offshore, adding to the lighthouse's natural charm.

For the local community and the broader population of Maine, Bass Harbor Head Lighthouse holds deep cultural significance. It is a symbol of resilience, standing strong against the Atlantic's relentless tides and storms. The lighthouse is part of the heritage of Mount Desert Island, where fishing has been a way of life for generations. It represents a connection to the sea and is a reminder of the region's maritime history, evoking nostalgia for a time when lighthouses were the primary means of ensuring safe passage for ships.

The lighthouse's location poses unique challenges. Its cliffside perch makes it vulnerable to erosion, and the constant exposure to saltwater spray accelerates the wear and tear on its structure. Maintenance is essential to preserving the lighthouse, which has been under the care of the National Park Service since it was added to Acadia National Park. Regular inspections and restorations help keep the lighthouse in excellent condition, allowing it to continue guiding ships while serving as a historic landmark.

LIGHTHOUSE: BEACON OF HISTORY AND LIGHT

An interesting fact about Bass Harbor Head Lighthouse is that it has become a staple of American coastal imagery. It has appeared on postcards, in magazines, and travel guides, capturing the essence of Maine's rugged coastline. Despite its fame, the lighthouse itself is relatively small, standing only about 10 meters tall. However, the cliffside location elevates it, allowing its light to reach far out into the ocean. This positioning is an ingenious use of natural elevation, making the lighthouse effective despite its modest height.

The lighthouse is essential to maritime safety in the region. Located at the entrance to Bass Harbor, it guides vessels around Mount Desert Island's southern tip, helping them avoid hazardous rocks and cliffs. Its red light, visible from miles away, warns ships of the shoreline, making it a critical asset for the U.S. Coast Guard, which operates the beacon. The lighthouse has witnessed changes in maritime technology over the decades, evolving from a manually lit beacon to an automated light, but its purpose remains the same—ensuring the safety of those at sea.

Visitors can reach Bass Harbor Head Lighthouse by car, as it is located within Acadia National Park, which is accessible by well-maintained roads. The nearby town of Bar Harbor provides additional transport options, including shuttle services that operate during the peak tourist season. Many travelers arrive via Bangor International Airport, which is the nearest major airport, and from there, they can take a scenic drive to Mount Desert Island. The lighthouse's proximity to Acadia National Park makes it a convenient stop for tourists exploring the area's natural beauty.

As dusk settles over Mount Desert Island, the Bass Harbor Head Lighthouse casts its red glow across the darkening waters, a steadfast presence on the rocky shore. It has seen generations of ships pass by, and its light has guided many safely home. For locals, visitors, and sailors alike, the lighthouse is a beloved landmark, a piece of Maine's soul preserved on the edge of the continent. Its story is one of resilience, natural beauty, and a deep connection to the sea, symbolizing the enduring spirit of New England's rugged coast.

8. Bell Rock Lighthouse - UK (Scotland)

Bell Rock Lighthouse, standing resolute amidst the treacherous waters of the North Sea, is a triumph of human ingenuity and engineering. Located about 11 miles off the coast of Angus, Scotland, this lighthouse was built atop the notorious Bell Rock, a reef submerged for most of the day and only exposed during low tide. Rising 35 meters above the relentless waves, this stone structure has withstood the test of time, safeguarding countless ships from the perilous waters that surround it. Its isolated location and the harsh environment make Bell Rock Lighthouse a remarkable feat, one of the oldest sea-washed lighthouses in existence.

Construction of the lighthouse began in 1807 under the direction of engineer Robert Stevenson, who faced incredible challenges in building on a submerged reef. The treacherous conditions and the limited time window during low tide added immense difficulty to the project. Workers had only a few hours each day to lay the foundation, and even then, they were at the mercy of the North Sea's unpredictable weather. Despite these challenges, the lighthouse was completed in 1811, an astonishing achievement in an era without modern machinery. Since its completion, the Bell Rock Lighthouse has become a symbol of resilience, a guardian against the dangers of the sea.

The climate in this part of Scotland is typical of the North Sea region, with cold winters, cool summers, and a persistent chill in the air brought by sea winds. Winters can be especially harsh, with temperatures often hovering around freezing, and strong gusts and heavy waves are a constant feature. In summer, temperatures rarely rise above 60°F (15°C), and misty or cloudy skies are frequent. These conditions emphasize the need for a sturdy, reliable structure, as the lighthouse must continue operating under all weather conditions to guide vessels safely past the hidden dangers of Bell Rock.

The lighthouse's beam has served as a crucial navigational aid for over two centuries, preventing shipwrecks on the reef that have claimed many lives and vessels throughout history. Even before the lighthouse was built, sailors knew of Bell Rock's dangers, with legends suggesting that a bell was once installed on the reef to warn passing ships. Though the bell was reportedly stolen by pirates, the lighthouse became its more permanent and effective successor, casting a light visible for miles across the dark, often foggy waters of the North Sea.

Despite its isolated location, Bell Rock Lighthouse has captured the fascination of many. It remains an iconic symbol in Scotland, representing the perseverance of those who built it and the bravery of the keepers who once manned it, facing weeks or months at a time in solitude. Today, the lighthouse is automated, but its legacy as a symbol of human determination remains strong. People from all over the world admire it, even if they can only view it from afar. It has inspired countless paintings, stories, and even maritime songs, cementing its place in Scottish culture.

Flora and fauna around Bell Rock are sparse due to the harsh marine environment. However, the surrounding waters are rich in marine life, with fish species that thrive in the cold currents of the North Sea. Seabirds are frequent visitors, with gulls, puffins, and cormorants often

LIGHTHOUSE: BEACON OF HISTORY AND LIGHT

seen circling above or perched on the rocks during low tide. Occasionally, seals and porpoises can be spotted in the waters near the lighthouse, adding a touch of life to the stark, windswept landscape.

Socially, Bell Rock Lighthouse has had a lasting impact, not just in Scotland but across maritime history. It has come to represent the determination and courage of those who venture into the unknown, willing to confront the unforgiving elements. The lighthouse is also a testament to Robert Stevenson's vision and the skills of those who built it under near-impossible conditions. In Scotland, it is a source of pride, embodying the resilience and spirit of the people who call this rugged land home.

The location of Bell Rock Lighthouse presents ongoing challenges. Maintenance of the lighthouse is difficult due to its remoteness and the rough seas surrounding it. Even though it has been automated since the late 20th century, regular inspections and upkeep are necessary to ensure that the light continues to function properly. Getting supplies and maintenance crews to the lighthouse requires careful planning, as weather conditions can make access impossible for days at a time. This isolation makes the lighthouse one of the most challenging to maintain in the world.

One fascinating fact about Bell Rock Lighthouse is that it was built using interlocking stones, a revolutionary technique at the time, designed to make the structure as strong and stable as possible. This technique has allowed it to withstand over two centuries of violent storms and crashing waves without any major structural issues. The construction is so durable that, to this day, it is one of the oldest sea-washed lighthouses still in operation. Additionally, the lighthouse's design influenced many other lighthouses built on dangerous reefs, making it a pioneering model in lighthouse engineering.

The importance of Bell Rock Lighthouse cannot be overstated. It is a beacon of safety, guiding countless vessels past one of Scotland's most dangerous reefs. The North Sea has long been a busy route for ships, and the lighthouse's light has been a welcome sight for sailors navigating the unpredictable waters. In its early years, the lighthouse was manned by keepers who braved the isolation to keep the light burning, a commitment that saved countless lives. Today, though its role has been partially overtaken by modern navigation technology, the lighthouse remains a critical landmark.

While reaching Bell Rock Lighthouse is not easy, it remains a significant point of reference for ships traveling through the North Sea. The closest mainland ports, such as those in Arbroath and Dundee, are where visitors can learn about the lighthouse and its history. While it isn't accessible to the public due to its dangerous location, the lighthouse is visible from certain vantage points along the coast, particularly during clear weather. Its striking presence on the water continues to draw the interest of historians, maritime enthusiasts, and travelers who admire its legacy from afar.

As night falls, Bell Rock Lighthouse stands resilient, casting its beam across the vast, dark expanse of the North Sea. For over 200 years, it has been a steadfast guardian, a symbol of strength against the wild forces of nature. For Scotland, it is more than just a lighthouse; it is a piece of heritage, a reminder of the courage and ingenuity that turned a dangerous reef into a beacon of safety. It is a story of triumph, resilience, and the enduring spirit of those who dared to build where few would tread. For all who see it, Bell Rock Lighthouse shines as a testament to the power of human determination.

9. Byron Bay Lighthouse - Australia

The Byron Bay Lighthouse, perched atop the cliffs of Cape Byron, holds the title of the easternmost lighthouse on the Australian mainland. Towering at a modest 22 meters, its whitewashed walls gleam under the bright Australian sun, making it a striking landmark against the vibrant blue of the Pacific Ocean. Located at Cape Byron, near the town of Byron Bay in New South Wales, this lighthouse has been a beacon for over a century, guiding ships safely along the rugged coastline.

Constructed in 1901, the lighthouse was built to address the dangers that Cape Byron presented to passing vessels. This area of the Pacific coast was well-traveled, but the jagged rocks and unpredictable weather posed significant risks to ships navigating close to shore. Designed by Charles Harding, the lighthouse was equipped with the most powerful lens of the time, enabling it to cast a beam visible up to 27 nautical miles. The powerful light provided much-needed assurance for sailors, becoming an essential part of the region's maritime safety.

Byron Bay enjoys a subtropical climate, with warm summers and mild winters. Temperatures average around 80°F (27°C) in summer and

60°F (15°C) in winter, with a humid atmosphere due to its coastal position. This mild weather makes the area a year-round destination, drawing visitors to both the lighthouse and the surrounding beaches. During the winter months, the waters near Cape Byron attract migrating humpback whales, offering a breathtaking sight for those who visit the lighthouse during this season. The whale migration has become an iconic part of the Byron Bay experience, with many visitors climbing up to the lighthouse to catch a glimpse of these majestic creatures.

Over the years, the Byron Bay Lighthouse has become one of Australia's most popular tourist attractions. Thousands of visitors come to experience the panoramic views from the lighthouse, with sweeping vistas of the coastline, lush hinterland, and the vast expanse of the Pacific Ocean. Its location on Cape Byron, with cliffs that drop steeply to the sea, makes it a perfect spot for watching both sunrise and sunset. The lighthouse itself is well-maintained and offers a picturesque setting, with its cylindrical tower and red-topped lantern contrasting beautifully with the natural surroundings.

The flora around Cape Byron and the lighthouse area includes coastal heathland, eucalyptus trees, and native shrubs adapted to the salt-rich environment. The cliffs are adorned with patches of vibrant wildflowers in the spring, adding color to the landscape. The area is also rich in fauna; aside from whales, visitors can spot dolphins in the nearby waters, and a variety of seabirds soar above the cliffs. The cliffs around the lighthouse are also home to lizards and other small reptiles, which bask in the sun on the rocky surfaces.

For the local community, the lighthouse represents a cherished part of Byron Bay's identity. It is a place where locals and tourists alike come to experience nature's beauty and gain a sense of the area's maritime history. The lighthouse's importance to the town cannot be understated; it has not only guided ships but also shaped Byron Bay's image as a destination of natural beauty and tranquility. The lighthouse

LIGHTHOUSE: BEACON OF HISTORY AND LIGHT

has also played a role in scientific research, particularly in studying marine life in the region, as it provides an elevated vantage point from which researchers can observe the ocean.

Located on a high cliff, the lighthouse is exposed to the full force of coastal winds and salt air, which can be harsh on the structure. Regular maintenance is required to preserve its exterior and ensure the functionality of the light. The salt-laden air has led to wear on the structure over time, necessitating periodic restoration work. However, thanks to efforts by local authorities and the community, the lighthouse has been well-preserved and continues to stand as a proud landmark.

A lesser-known fact about the Byron Bay Lighthouse is its connection to early radio communication in Australia. In the early 20th century, it played a role in the development of maritime radio, which was used to communicate with passing ships. This added an extra layer of security, allowing ships to receive weather updates and other essential information as they passed by Cape Byron. The lighthouse's contribution to maritime safety extended beyond just its beam; it became a part of a larger network of navigational aids and communication tools that ensured safer journeys along the Australian coast.

The significance of Byron Bay Lighthouse goes beyond its function as a navigational aid. It has become a cultural icon, embodying Australia's connection to the sea and the land's natural beauty. For Indigenous Australians, Cape Byron and the surrounding areas hold cultural significance, and the lighthouse stands on land that has been part of their heritage for thousands of years. Today, the lighthouse area includes interpretive displays and educational programs, which acknowledge this history and share it with visitors from around the world.

Visitors can reach Byron Bay Lighthouse by various modes of transport. The lighthouse is easily accessible by road from Byron Bay, and a walking trail leads up to the site, offering beautiful views along the way. Public transport, including buses, operates from nearby towns, and during peak tourist season, shuttles provide convenient access for those who prefer not to drive. Byron Bay is also a short drive from Ballina Byron Gateway Airport, which connects the area to other major Australian cities, making it a popular stop for both domestic and international travelers.

As evening falls and the sky darkens, the Byron Bay Lighthouse stands illuminated, casting its beam across the waters of the Pacific. It has witnessed countless sunrises and sunsets, marking the easternmost point of Australia with a light that has guided and inspired generations. For locals and visitors alike, the lighthouse is more than just a beacon; it is a place of reflection, a reminder of the beauty of nature, and a testament to the enduring connection between the land and the sea. Its story is woven into the fabric of Byron Bay, embodying the spirit of a place where history, culture, and natural wonder converge.

10. Cabo da Roca Lighthouse - Portugal

The Cabo da Roca Lighthouse, perched at the westernmost point of mainland Europe, stands as a sentinel on the rugged cliffs of Portugal's Atlantic coast. Overlooking the vast ocean, this lighthouse has guided sailors since its establishment in 1772, marking a point that explorers once considered the edge of the known world. Rising 22 meters above the ground and over 150 meters above sea level, it has become a beloved landmark, drawing visitors from around the world to experience its dramatic setting and historical significance.

Constructed by order of the Marquis of Pombal, the lighthouse was initially built as part of Portugal's efforts to improve maritime safety during the Age of Exploration. Cabo da Roca's strategic location made it ideal for a beacon that could help ships avoid the dangerous cliffs and navigate the busy shipping routes along Portugal's western coast. Over the centuries, the lighthouse has been updated with modern technology, transitioning from oil lamps to electric lights, but it has retained its original charm, with its white walls and red lantern room standing as a symbol of resilience against the powerful Atlantic winds.

Located in the Sintra-Cascais Natural Park, Cabo da Roca experiences a Mediterranean climate, tempered by the ocean's influence. Summers are warm, with average temperatures around 77°F (25°C), and winters are mild, rarely dipping below 50°F (10°C). The coastal weather brings strong winds year-round, and fog often envelops the cliffs, adding an air of mystique to the lighthouse. These conditions make it both a challenging and rewarding destination, where visitors can witness the raw beauty of the Atlantic and the dramatic cliffs that plunge down to the sea below.

Today, the Cabo da Roca Lighthouse is a popular attraction, with tourists flocking to the cape to take in the panoramic views and visit this historic site. The lighthouse grounds are surrounded by rugged coastal vegetation, including hardy shrubs and wildflowers that bloom in spring, adding vibrant colors to the landscape. The area is home to a variety of bird species, such as gulls and hawks, which are often seen soaring above the cliffs. The ecosystem around Cabo da Roca is well-adapted to the salty, windy environment, creating a natural habitat that complements the lighthouse's stoic presence.

For the people of Portugal, Cabo da Roca Lighthouse holds a special place in the nation's maritime heritage. It symbolizes the spirit of exploration that defined Portugal during the Age of Discovery, a time when Portuguese navigators ventured into uncharted waters and opened new routes across the globe. The lighthouse is more than a navigational aid; it is a tribute to Portugal's rich history and its connection to the sea, resonating with locals and tourists alike who come to admire this national icon.

However, the lighthouse's location on the edge of the continent poses significant challenges. Exposed to the full force of Atlantic storms, it must endure high winds, heavy rain, and corrosive salt air. Regular maintenance is necessary to protect its structure, and the National Maritime Authority oversees its preservation, ensuring that it continues to shine brightly as a beacon of safety. Despite these efforts,

LIGHTHOUSE: BEACON OF HISTORY AND LIGHT

the lighthouse's remote position makes upkeep a constant challenge, as repairs must be carefully timed to avoid the worst of the weather.

One interesting fact about the Cabo da Roca Lighthouse is that it marks the place described by the 16th-century poet Luís de Camões as "where the land ends and the sea begins." This poetic description has become a well-known phrase in Portugal, capturing the essence of the location and the lighthouse's symbolic role as the guardian of Europe's western edge. It is a place where land meets the infinite ocean, evoking a sense of awe and reverence for the natural forces that shape the coast.

The lighthouse's importance extends far beyond its role as a navigational aid. It is a cultural and historical landmark, embodying Portugal's legacy of maritime exploration. Positioned on a cape that has witnessed centuries of maritime history, the lighthouse has been a constant, steady presence for ships traversing the Atlantic. Its beam, visible up to 26 nautical miles away, has guided countless vessels, protecting them from the hidden dangers of the rocky coastline and ensuring safe passage along Portugal's western shores.

Visitors can reach the Cabo da Roca Lighthouse by car or bus from Lisbon, which is about a 40-minute drive away. The journey offers scenic views of the Portuguese countryside, and the nearby towns of Sintra and Cascais provide additional transportation options for tourists. During peak travel season, buses and tours from Lisbon bring visitors directly to Cabo da Roca, making it accessible for both local and international travelers. The nearby hiking trails also draw nature enthusiasts, as the area around the lighthouse offers some of the most breathtaking views in Portugal.

As the sun dips below the horizon and the lighthouse casts its light over the vast Atlantic, Cabo da Roca stands as a timeless testament to Portugal's heritage. The lighthouse has seen generations of explorers, fishermen, and travelers pass by, each one drawn to the rugged beauty of this remote cape. For all who visit, the Cabo da Roca Lighthouse is a place of reflection, a reminder of Portugal's enduring connection to the sea and the courage of those who once sailed into the unknown. It is a beacon of history, culture, and natural splendor, shining brightly at the very edge of the continent.

11. Cabo de São Vicente Lighthouse - Portugal

The Cabo de São Vicente Lighthouse stands defiantly on the windswept cliffs of Portugal's southwestern coast, a beacon of safety for vessels navigating the treacherous waters of the Atlantic. Located near the town of Sagres, at the southwestern tip of mainland Europe, this lighthouse marks one of the most important maritime routes in Europe, guiding ships as they pass the rugged cliffs of Cabo de São Vicente, where land meets the vastness of the ocean. The red and white tower is perched on cliffs that rise over 75 meters above the sea, offering breathtaking views of the Atlantic stretching endlessly toward the horizon.

The first lighthouse at Cabo de São Vicente was built in 1846, replacing a small beacon that had been used since the 16th century. This location had been known as a sacred site even in ancient times, often referred to as the "end of the world." Mariners once feared this corner of the coast, where powerful currents, high waves, and strong winds made navigation difficult. Recognizing the need for a reliable beacon to guide ships around this critical point, the Portuguese government commissioned the construction of a larger, more powerful lighthouse, which has since been modernized to continue serving as a vital aid to navigation.

The area surrounding Cabo de São Vicente experiences a mild Mediterranean climate, with warm, dry summers and cool, wet winters. Summer temperatures often reach around 80°F (27°C), while winter temperatures hover around 55°F (13°C). The lighthouse is frequently exposed to strong winds from the Atlantic, and storms are not uncommon, especially during the winter months. These weather conditions add to the dramatic atmosphere of the location, where the sound of waves crashing against the cliffs resonates in the air.

The Cabo de São Vicente Lighthouse has become a popular attraction for tourists visiting the Algarve region. Known for its striking coastal views, this lighthouse attracts visitors eager to experience the raw beauty of Portugal's western coast. The site is particularly popular at sunset, when the sky is painted with hues of orange and pink, and the sun dips below the Atlantic, casting a golden glow over the ocean and the cliffs. The lighthouse, silhouetted against the setting sun, creates an unforgettable scene that captures the spirit of this remote, powerful place.

The landscape around the lighthouse is covered with coastal vegetation, including hardy shrubs, wildflowers, and low-lying plants adapted to the salty air and rocky soil. In spring, vibrant wildflowers add color to the cliffs, creating a striking contrast against the rugged rocks and deep blue of the ocean. The area is home to various bird species, such as gulls, cormorants, and peregrine falcons that nest along the cliffs. Marine life is abundant in the surrounding waters, with dolphins occasionally seen in the waves below, adding to the natural allure of this iconic site.

For the people of Portugal, the Cabo de São Vicente Lighthouse is not only a navigational aid but also a symbol of the nation's rich maritime heritage. This area, steeped in history, was once a launching point for

LIGHTHOUSE: BEACON OF HISTORY AND LIGHT

Portuguese explorers during the Age of Discovery. The lighthouse stands as a reminder of the adventurous spirit that led Portuguese navigators to chart the unknown seas, and for locals, it is a point of pride that represents Portugal's enduring connection to the ocean. It has become a cultural landmark, embodying the resilience of the people who call this coast home.

The lighthouse's isolated position on the cliffs presents numerous challenges. Constant exposure to salt air and high winds accelerates the wear and tear on the structure, requiring regular maintenance to preserve its functionality. Additionally, the cliffs themselves are subject to erosion, which is carefully monitored to prevent any impact on the lighthouse. Despite these challenges, the lighthouse remains in excellent condition, thanks to ongoing preservation efforts by the Portuguese authorities who recognize its importance to both navigation and cultural heritage.

A lesser-known fact about the Cabo de São Vicente Lighthouse is its powerful lens, one of the strongest in Europe, which allows its light to be seen from as far as 32 nautical miles away. The beacon's strength has made it an essential aid for vessels traveling along this part of the Atlantic coast. The lighthouse's rotating beam has helped countless ships avoid the dangerous reefs and navigate safely around the cape, making it one of the most significant lighthouses in Europe.

Beyond its practical importance, the lighthouse holds symbolic significance. Its presence at the southwestern edge of the continent has made it a pilgrimage site for those who appreciate Portugal's historical role in maritime exploration. Standing at the edge of the cliffs, one can imagine the awe of explorers who set sail from this very point, venturing into uncharted waters. Today, visitors continue to feel a sense of wonder at the vastness of the ocean and the lighthouse's role as a guardian of the coast, embodying both history and the indomitable spirit of exploration.

Travelers can access Cabo de São Vicente Lighthouse by car, with well-maintained roads leading from nearby Sagres. Buses also connect Sagres with other parts of the Algarve, making it accessible for both domestic and international tourists. Faro Airport, located about 120 kilometers away, provides the nearest major transportation hub, with connections to cities across Europe. This convenient access has contributed to the lighthouse's popularity as a tourist destination, and its dramatic setting makes it a must-see for those exploring the Algarve. As dusk falls and the beam from the lighthouse sweeps across the Atlantic, Cabo de São Vicente remains a steadfast presence on the edge of Europe. For centuries, it has been a beacon of hope and safety, guiding ships through the challenging waters of the western coast. The lighthouse's story is one of resilience, adventure, and an enduring connection to the sea. It stands as a tribute to Portugal's maritime legacy and the courage of those who once saw this cape as the edge of the known world. Today, it continues to inspire awe in those who visit, a reminder of the power and beauty of the natural world and the remarkable history of human exploration.

12. Cape Agulhas Lighthouse - South Africa

The Cape Agulhas Lighthouse stands proudly at the southernmost tip of Africa, where the Atlantic and Indian Oceans meet in a dramatic confluence of waves and wind. This red-and-white striped beacon, built in 1849, is South Africa's second-oldest working lighthouse and one of the most iconic landmarks on the continent. Rising to a height of 27 meters, it was designed to guide sailors around the treacherous waters of Cape Agulhas, a region infamous for shipwrecks caused by unpredictable currents, submerged rocks, and shifting sands.

The decision to build a lighthouse at Cape Agulhas came in response to a growing need for navigational aids along South Africa's coastline. During the 19th century, maritime traffic around the Cape was heavy, with ships traveling between Europe, the East Indies, and the Americas. The rocky coast, combined with powerful oceanic currents, made navigation hazardous, and many vessels met their fate in these unforgiving waters. In response, the South African government commissioned the construction of the Cape Agulhas Lighthouse, modeled after the ancient Pharos of Alexandria in Egypt, adding a touch of historical grandeur to its utilitarian purpose.

Located on the edge of the African continent, Cape Agulhas experiences a Mediterranean climate with moderate, cool temperatures year-round. Summers are mild, averaging around 68°F (20°C), while winters can drop to about 50°F (10°C). The region is often buffeted by strong winds, especially in the winter months, which bring choppy seas and a misty haze that hangs over the horizon. This ever-changing climate creates an atmosphere of raw beauty around the lighthouse, with bright, clear days showcasing the deep blue of the ocean and overcast, windy days enhancing the lighthouse's lonely resilience.

Cape Agulhas Lighthouse is a popular destination for travelers who venture to this remote corner of South Africa to witness the meeting point of two mighty oceans. The lighthouse grounds offer panoramic views of the rugged coastline, where visitors can gaze out over the endless expanse of water and feel the thrill of standing at the edge of a continent. Inside, the lighthouse features a small museum with exhibits detailing the area's maritime history and the role the lighthouse has played in protecting seafarers. Visitors can climb the narrow staircase to the top, where they are rewarded with breathtaking views that stretch out over both oceans.

The surrounding landscape is defined by coastal vegetation adapted to the harsh, salty air and rocky soil. The flora includes hardy shrubs, grasses, and flowering plants that add vibrant touches of green and yellow to the otherwise stark terrain. Cape Agulhas is also rich in wildlife, particularly bird species that thrive in the coastal environment. Gulls, cormorants, and oystercatchers are frequent visitors, filling the air with their calls as they soar above the waves. Occasionally, dolphins can be spotted swimming offshore, and during the winter months, migrating whales pass by the cape, creating an awe-inspiring sight for those lucky enough to witness it.

LIGHTHOUSE: BEACON OF HISTORY AND LIGHT

For the people of South Africa, the Cape Agulhas Lighthouse is more than just a navigational aid; it is a cultural and historical symbol. It represents the determination and ingenuity of the early settlers who built this structure to protect ships navigating one of the world's most dangerous coastal routes. The lighthouse has become a symbol of South Africa's maritime heritage, and its red and white stripes are instantly recognizable. It has also played an important role in educating the public about the significance of Cape Agulhas as a geographic and maritime landmark.

The location of Cape Agulhas Lighthouse poses unique challenges, particularly in terms of maintenance. The structure is exposed to high winds and salty ocean spray, which accelerate the weathering of its exterior. Regular upkeep is necessary to protect the lighthouse from the harsh coastal environment, and local authorities ensure that it remains in good condition for future generations to appreciate. The remote location also makes access difficult, especially during bad weather, adding another layer of complexity to the task of preserving this iconic structure.

A lesser-known fact about the Cape Agulhas Lighthouse is that it marks the official dividing line between the Atlantic and Indian Oceans, a geographical distinction that is celebrated with a plaque on the cliffs nearby. For sailors, this boundary has significant implications, as it denotes a shift in ocean currents, water temperature, and marine life. The waters on the Atlantic side are generally colder, while the Indian Ocean brings warmer currents, creating a unique confluence at Cape Agulhas that has fascinated scientists and oceanographers for centuries.

The importance of Cape Agulhas Lighthouse extends far beyond its function as a warning beacon. It has served as a navigational aid for generations of sailors, guiding them through one of the most perilous sections of the African coast. Its beam, visible for miles, has helped countless vessels avoid the hidden dangers that lurk beneath the waves.

The lighthouse is an enduring symbol of safety and security, a reassuring presence for those who brave the open sea. Its role in maritime safety has cemented its place in South African history, and it continues to serve as a reminder of the challenges and triumphs of exploration.

Access to Cape Agulhas Lighthouse is relatively straightforward, with well-maintained roads connecting it to nearby towns such as Bredasdorp and Struisbaai. The closest major city is Cape Town, from which visitors can take a scenic drive along the coast, passing through charming coastal towns and picturesque landscapes. Local tour operators offer guided trips to the lighthouse, providing visitors with insights into its history and significance. The region is also popular for road trips, and the lighthouse serves as a unique stop for those exploring the beauty of South Africa's southern coast.

As night falls and the beam of Cape Agulhas Lighthouse sweeps across the darkened waters, this iconic structure stands as a symbol of resilience and endurance. For over 170 years, it has withstood the forces of nature, guiding ships and inspiring those who come to marvel at its beauty. The lighthouse at Cape Agulhas is more than just a building; it is a testament to the courage and vision of those who built it, a beacon of hope for sailors navigating the southern seas, and a symbol of South Africa's connection to the ocean. Standing at the meeting point of two oceans, it captures the essence of a place where nature's power meets human ingenuity, a true landmark of the African continent.

13. Cape Byron Lighthouse - Australia

Cape Byron Lighthouse, perched on the easternmost point of the Australian mainland, offers a stunning view of the Pacific Ocean from its cliffside position in Byron Bay, New South Wales. Built in 1901, this lighthouse stands as a symbol of maritime heritage, guiding ships and travelers alike for over a century. At 22 meters tall, its white cylindrical tower with a red-topped lantern contrasts beautifully against the vast blue of the ocean and sky. The lighthouse sits high on a cliff, giving it a natural elevation that amplifies its light, making it one of the most visible lighthouses along the eastern coast of Australia.

The history of Cape Byron Lighthouse is steeped in the early 20th-century need for improved maritime safety. Cape Byron's location is crucial for ships navigating the coastline, but the region's rocky shores and frequent storms made this area particularly treacherous. The decision to build a lighthouse here was driven by the increasing maritime traffic, and Charles Harding, a prominent architect of the time, was commissioned to design a structure that would endure the harsh coastal conditions. Since then, the Cape Byron Lighthouse has served as a vital navigational aid, initially using kerosene lamps and later upgrading to electric light.

Byron Bay experiences a subtropical climate, with warm, humid summers and mild, pleasant winters. The summer temperatures range from 77°F to 86°F (25°C to 30°C), while winter temperatures remain around 59°F (15°C). This temperate weather, combined with the ocean breeze, makes Cape Byron a year-round destination. During the winter, migrating humpback whales pass by the cape, attracting visitors who come to witness the spectacular sight from the lighthouse vantage point. The whale migration has become a seasonal highlight, reinforcing the lighthouse's role not only as a guide but also as a place of natural beauty.

Today, Cape Byron Lighthouse is one of Australia's most iconic and frequently visited landmarks. Thousands of visitors come to marvel at the view, hike the nearby trails, and experience the natural beauty of the coastline. The lighthouse provides panoramic views, especially at sunrise, when the first rays of light illuminate the cliffs and ocean below. Visitors can tour the lighthouse grounds, which include a small museum showcasing the region's maritime history and the lighthouse's role in protecting ships. Climbing to the top offers an unparalleled view of the coastline, allowing visitors to see miles of pristine beaches and lush hinterland.

The flora around Cape Byron is a blend of coastal heathland, eucalyptus forests, and flowering native shrubs. The cliffs are home to hardy vegetation that thrives in the salty air and wind, and during spring, wildflowers add bursts of color to the landscape. The area's fauna is equally vibrant; aside from the migrating whales, dolphins are often seen frolicking in the waves below, and a variety of seabirds, including gulls and pelicans, frequent the cliffs. The region's biodiversity is protected within the Cape Byron State Conservation Area, which aims to preserve the natural environment surrounding the lighthouse.

LIGHTHOUSE: BEACON OF HISTORY AND LIGHT

For the local community and Australians in general, Cape Byron Lighthouse is a symbol of resilience and historical significance. It embodies the spirit of coastal living, a place where land meets the vastness of the ocean. The lighthouse also serves as a point of pride for the town of Byron Bay, which has grown from a quiet seaside community into a popular tourist destination. The lighthouse's presence has influenced Byron Bay's identity, making it a symbol of exploration, safety, and the appreciation of nature's beauty.

The lighthouse's location on a cliff presents maintenance challenges due to constant exposure to salt air and strong winds. Regular inspections and repairs are essential to counteract the wear and tear caused by the harsh coastal conditions. The lighthouse is managed by the Australian Maritime Safety Authority, which ensures that it continues to operate effectively. Its remote position also requires careful coordination for maintenance work, as access is limited, especially during periods of high winds or rough seas.

A fascinating aspect of Cape Byron Lighthouse is its role in early communication technology. In its early years, the lighthouse was equipped with a signal station to communicate with passing ships, a feature that added an extra layer of safety. Over time, as radio technology advanced, the signal station became obsolete, yet it marked Cape Byron as a pioneer in maritime communication for Australia. Today, while the lighthouse no longer relies on these early communication methods, its history of innovation remains an intriguing part of its legacy.

The importance of Cape Byron Lighthouse cannot be overstated. Positioned at a critical juncture on the coast, it has provided a guiding light for countless vessels, helping them navigate the rugged shores and avoid dangerous waters. Its beam, visible from miles away, is a testament to the safety and security it has offered for over a century. Even with the advent of GPS and modern navigation systems, the lighthouse continues to serve as a backup aid, symbolizing the enduring value of traditional navigational tools.

Visitors to Cape Byron Lighthouse have various travel options. Byron Bay is accessible by road from Brisbane, Sydney, and other major cities, making it a popular stop on road trips along Australia's east coast. Additionally, Ballina Byron Gateway Airport is a short drive away, providing connections to other parts of Australia. Local buses and shuttle services operate from the Byron Bay town center, and for those who prefer an active approach, hiking trails lead up to the lighthouse, offering scenic views along the way.

As the sun sets and Cape Byron Lighthouse casts its light across the ocean, it stands as a beacon of history, nature, and resilience. For over a century, it has watched over the coastline, its light guiding ships and its presence inspiring all who visit. Cape Byron Lighthouse is more than just a navigational tool; it is a place of wonder, where people come to connect with the sea and experience the vast beauty of the Australian landscape. The lighthouse remains a cherished landmark, embodying the spirit of Byron Bay and the timeless allure of the coast.

14. Cape Hatteras Lighthouse - USA

Cape Hatteras Lighthouse stands proudly on the shifting sands of North Carolina's Outer Banks, a towering black and white sentinel with a distinctive spiral pattern. At 63 meters (207 feet), it is the tallest brick lighthouse in the United States, and its striking design makes it one of the most recognizable beacons in the world. The lighthouse, situated on Hatteras Island, has been a crucial guide for mariners navigating the treacherous waters off Cape Hatteras, an area known ominously as the "Graveyard of the Atlantic."

The history of Cape Hatteras Lighthouse dates back to 1803 when the first version was built to address the need for navigational aids along this dangerous stretch of coast. The treacherous currents and unpredictable storms off the coast had claimed many ships, making the construction of a lighthouse essential. However, this initial lighthouse was soon found inadequate, and in 1870, the current, taller lighthouse was constructed to better serve the maritime community. Its powerful light was visible for 20 miles out to sea, providing a much-needed beacon for sailors navigating these perilous waters.

Cape Hatteras, located along the eastern edge of the United States, experiences a coastal climate with hot, humid summers and mild winters. Temperatures in the summer can reach 85°F (29°C), while winter temperatures average around 50°F (10°C). The area is frequently exposed to storms, especially during the Atlantic hurricane season, which can bring powerful winds and heavy rains to the region. This stormy weather has had a significant impact on the lighthouse and the surrounding landscape, leading to ongoing challenges with erosion that have threatened the lighthouse's stability over the years.

The Cape Hatteras Lighthouse is a beloved landmark and a popular destination for visitors to the Outer Banks. Every year, thousands of tourists come to climb its 257 steps to the top, where they are rewarded with stunning panoramic views of the Atlantic Ocean and the sweeping sands of Hatteras Island. The lighthouse is also a favorite subject for photographers and artists, and its iconic black-and-white spiral design has become a symbol of the Outer Banks. Visitors are drawn not only to its beauty but also to its rich history and the role it has played in ensuring maritime safety for over a century.

The lighthouse is surrounded by a unique coastal ecosystem, with sandy dunes, grasses, and shrubs that are adapted to the harsh conditions of the Outer Banks. Native vegetation, including sea oats and American beach grass, helps to stabilize the dunes and protect the area from erosion. The waters near Cape Hatteras are teeming with marine life, attracting dolphins, sea turtles, and a variety of fish species. The area is also home to diverse birdlife, with seabirds such as gulls, pelicans, and osprey frequently seen flying over the dunes and fishing in the waters below.

For the people of North Carolina, the Cape Hatteras Lighthouse holds a special place in their hearts. It represents the strength and resilience of the local community, which has weathered countless storms and hurricanes over the years. The lighthouse has become a cultural symbol, embodying the maritime heritage of the region and serving as a

LIGHTHOUSE: BEACON OF HISTORY AND LIGHT

reminder of the many lives it has helped to protect. Its presence on the Outer Banks has shaped the identity of the area, drawing people from all over the world to experience its beauty and history.

The lighthouse's location on a sandy barrier island poses unique challenges, particularly due to erosion. Over the years, the relentless force of the Atlantic has gradually worn away the shoreline, bringing the ocean dangerously close to the lighthouse. By the late 20th century, erosion had become so severe that the lighthouse was at risk of being lost to the sea. In an extraordinary feat of engineering, the entire lighthouse was moved inland in 1999, traveling nearly 2,900 feet to its current location. This move, known as the "Move of the Century," saved the lighthouse from the encroaching waves and preserved it for future generations.

One lesser-known fact about Cape Hatteras Lighthouse is that its distinctive black and white spiral design, known as a "daymark," was specifically chosen to make it more visible during the day. Each lighthouse along the Outer Banks has a unique daymark pattern, allowing sailors to distinguish them from one another. The Cape Hatteras Lighthouse's spirals are particularly effective in catching the eye, making it one of the most recognizable lighthouses on the coast.

The importance of Cape Hatteras Lighthouse cannot be overstated. Situated along the Atlantic coast, it has provided a guiding light for generations of sailors, helping them avoid the dangerous shoals and sandbars that have claimed many ships. The waters around Cape Hatteras are notoriously difficult to navigate, with shifting sands, strong currents, and frequent storms. The lighthouse's powerful beam, visible from great distances, has been a lifesaving presence for those at sea, marking a safe passage and warning of hidden dangers.

Getting to Cape Hatteras Lighthouse is an adventure in itself. Visitors can reach the Outer Banks by car, crossing a series of bridges that connect the islands to the mainland. The nearest airport is Norfolk International Airport in Virginia, and from there, it's a scenic drive through coastal North Carolina to reach Hatteras Island. Ferries also operate between the Outer Banks islands, providing a unique way for visitors to explore the region and experience the natural beauty of this remote part of the United States.

As the sun sets and the beam of Cape Hatteras Lighthouse sweeps across the horizon, it remains a steadfast symbol of hope and resilience. For over a century, it has stood guard over one of the most dangerous stretches of the Atlantic, protecting sailors and preserving lives. Cape Hatteras Lighthouse is more than just a structure; it is a testament to human ingenuity, a piece of history, and an enduring icon of the Outer Banks. For all who visit, it serves as a reminder of the power of the sea and the importance of those who work to keep it safe.

15. Cape Leeuwin Lighthouse - Australia

Cape Leeuwin Lighthouse stands proudly on the rocky peninsula at the southwestern tip of Australia, where the Indian and Southern Oceans collide. Built in 1895, this towering white lighthouse rises 39 meters (128 feet) above the cliffs and is Western Australia's tallest lighthouse. Its isolated position on Cape Leeuwin, near the town of Augusta, places it in a dramatic setting known for powerful waves and relentless winds. The lighthouse serves as a crucial beacon, guiding ships through the turbulent waters at one of the country's most significant maritime intersections.

The decision to construct the Cape Leeuwin Lighthouse stemmed from the increased maritime activity in the area and the hazards posed by Cape Leeuwin's unpredictable waters. Throughout the 19th century, as global trade routes developed, more ships navigated Australia's coastlines, and the dangerous conditions at Cape Leeuwin became evident. The lighthouse was built to protect these vessels, marking a key point in the treacherous journey around Australia's southern coast. With its beacon visible from 25 nautical miles, Cape Leeuwin

Lighthouse became a vital safeguard against the perils of the Southern Ocean.

The climate at Cape Leeuwin is classified as Mediterranean, with mild, wet winters and warm, dry summers. Temperatures range from around 77°F (25°C) in summer to 54°F (12°C) in winter. The lighthouse is frequently exposed to powerful westerly winds, which bring rain and heavy seas, especially during the winter months. These conditions lend the lighthouse an atmosphere of wild beauty, as its sturdy structure endures the elements year-round. During stormy days, waves crash against the rocks below, and mist from the ocean sometimes envelops the lighthouse, creating a scene both breathtaking and foreboding.

Today, Cape Leeuwin Lighthouse is a popular destination for travelers exploring Western Australia's coastline. Thousands of visitors come each year to stand at the edge of the continent and witness the merging of two oceans. The site offers panoramic views of the coastline, where visitors can watch as the turquoise waters of the Indian Ocean blend with the colder, deeper hues of the Southern Ocean. Climbing to the top of the lighthouse provides an even more expansive view, offering a rare perspective on the vastness of the sea.

The landscape surrounding Cape Leeuwin Lighthouse is dominated by coastal heathland, with native shrubs, wildflowers, and hardy grasses. The vegetation, adapted to the salt-rich air and rocky soil, bursts into color in spring, adding vibrancy to the windswept cliffs. The lighthouse is part of the Leeuwin-Naturaliste National Park, an area rich in biodiversity. Marine life in the waters includes dolphins and migrating humpback whales, which can be seen breaching offshore during their annual migration. The area is also a haven for seabirds, with cormorants, gulls, and albatrosses often spotted near the cliffs.

For the local community and Australians as a whole, Cape Leeuwin Lighthouse is more than just a navigational aid; it is a cultural symbol and a point of pride. It represents the resilience and determination of those who built it and those who maintained it in the face of harsh

LIGHTHOUSE: BEACON OF HISTORY AND LIGHT

conditions. The lighthouse has become an iconic landmark, embodying the adventurous spirit of Western Australia's coastal heritage. It also plays an educational role, as the on-site interpretive center provides insights into the history of the region and the lighthouse's enduring importance.

The remote location and harsh environment of Cape Leeuwin pose unique challenges for the lighthouse's maintenance. Constant exposure to salt air, strong winds, and occasional storms accelerates the weathering of its exterior, necessitating regular upkeep to preserve its iconic appearance. Despite these challenges, the Australian Maritime Safety Authority ensures that the lighthouse remains operational, upholding its role as both a historical landmark and a functional navigational aid.

One fascinating fact about Cape Leeuwin Lighthouse is its role in the maritime climate observations for Australia. The lighthouse's position at the meeting point of two major ocean currents makes it an ideal location for climate studies and weather observation, contributing valuable data to meteorological research. Its strategic location also allows scientists to monitor ocean temperatures and currents, which are critical for understanding broader climate patterns.

Cape Leeuwin Lighthouse holds significant importance for sailors navigating the southern seas. For generations, its powerful light has served as a warning of the nearby cliffs and rocks, ensuring the safety of ships traveling along Australia's coast. Even with modern navigation systems, the lighthouse remains a critical reference point, symbolizing the timeless value of traditional aids to navigation. Its presence at this crossroads of oceans highlights its role as a guardian of the southern waters.

Visitors to Cape Leeuwin Lighthouse have various travel options. The lighthouse is accessible by car from Perth, located about 300 kilometers to the north, and the journey offers scenic views of Western Australia's coastline. Local tour operators offer guided visits to the lighthouse, providing historical context and highlighting the area's natural beauty. Nearby airports, such as Busselton Margaret River Airport, offer additional access, making the lighthouse an accessible stop for both domestic and international travelers.

As the sun dips below the horizon and Cape Leeuwin Lighthouse casts its light across the vast ocean, it remains a steadfast symbol of Australia's maritime legacy. For over a century, it has stood as a beacon of safety and endurance, guarding the waters where two oceans meet. Cape Leeuwin Lighthouse is more than just a structure; it is a reminder of Australia's connection to the sea and the resilience required to thrive in this rugged, remote part of the world. For those who visit, it offers a glimpse into the history, beauty, and spirit of Western Australia's coastal wilderness.

16. Cape Otway Lighthouse - Australia

Cape Otway Lighthouse, perched on the southern coast of Victoria, Australia, is one of the country's oldest and most iconic lighthouses. Built in 1848, it stands 20 meters tall and has served as a vital beacon for ships navigating the perilous waters of the Bass Strait. Its cylindrical white tower, set against the wild expanse of the Southern Ocean, has been guiding mariners for over 170 years. Located on a dramatic, windswept cliff at the edge of Cape Otway, the lighthouse is a landmark with historical, cultural, and environmental significance.

The construction of Cape Otway Lighthouse was a response to the high number of shipwrecks occurring along Victoria's treacherous southern coastline. The Bass Strait, lying between the Australian mainland and Tasmania, is infamous for its strong winds, unpredictable currents, and dangerous reefs, which created a graveyard of shipwrecks throughout the 19th century. After numerous tragedies, the need for a lighthouse became apparent, and Cape Otway was chosen for its strategic position at the entrance to the strait. The lighthouse was constructed using local sandstone, quarried from the area, and its first light was lit in 1848, becoming one of Australia's first lighthouses to operate.

Cape Otway is known for its cool, temperate climate, with mild summers and cool, damp winters. Summer temperatures generally reach around 70°F (21°C), while winter temperatures average around 50°F (10°C). The coastal climate brings frequent winds, with fog and mist often rolling in from the ocean. This atmospheric weather adds to the lighthouse's charm, casting an air of mystery and beauty over the landscape, while also highlighting the rugged nature of the environment in which it was built. The climate conditions have made the lighthouse a striking landmark for visitors who come to witness both the beauty and the power of nature in this remote part of Australia.

Cape Otway Lighthouse has become a popular tourist destination, attracting visitors eager to explore the history and scenic beauty of the region. The site offers a range of activities, including guided tours of the lighthouse, educational exhibits, and viewing platforms that provide breathtaking views of the coast and ocean. The lighthouse also serves as a prime location for whale watching during migration season, when humpback and southern right whales pass through the waters off Cape Otway. Climbing to the top of the lighthouse provides a unique vantage point, offering sweeping views of the coastline, the surrounding national park, and the endless expanse of the ocean.

The area around the lighthouse is part of the Great Otway National Park, known for its diverse flora and fauna. The coastal heathland is home to a variety of native plants, including coastal tea trees, grasses, and wildflowers that add color to the landscape. The park is rich in wildlife, with koalas, kangaroos, and echidnas frequently spotted near the lighthouse grounds. Birdlife is abundant, with species such as cockatoos, parrots, and seabirds adding to the area's vibrant ecosystem. The combination of coastal vegetation and native wildlife makes Cape

LIGHTHOUSE: BEACON OF HISTORY AND LIGHT

Otway a place where visitors can experience the beauty of Australia's natural environment.

For the local community and Australians in general, Cape Otway Lighthouse is a symbol of resilience and a testament to the early efforts to protect maritime travelers. It has become an enduring part of Victoria's heritage, representing the courage and determination of those who braved the wilds of the southern coast to ensure the safety of ships and their passengers. The lighthouse has also influenced the identity of the region, drawing both tourists and locals to a site that has become iconic in Australian coastal culture.

The remote location of Cape Otway Lighthouse has posed unique challenges throughout its history. Maintaining the lighthouse in such an isolated and rugged setting required immense dedication from the lighthouse keepers and their families, who lived on-site and endured the harsh weather conditions. Today, the lighthouse is automated, but the environmental conditions still necessitate regular maintenance to protect it from erosion and weathering caused by the salt-laden sea air. The ongoing preservation efforts by local authorities ensure that this historic structure remains in excellent condition, preserving its legacy for future generations.

One lesser-known fact about Cape Otway Lighthouse is its role in the early telegraph network in Australia. In the 19th century, a telegraph station was established at Cape Otway, which connected with ships as they approached the coast. This telegraph station enabled faster communication with passing vessels, enhancing the safety of maritime travel. Today, the remains of the telegraph station can still be seen near the lighthouse, offering visitors a glimpse into this lesser-known aspect of the site's history and its importance in early communication technology.

Cape Otway Lighthouse is one of Australia's most important navigational landmarks. Its light served as a crucial guide for vessels traveling through the Bass Strait, helping them avoid the hazards posed by rocky outcrops and reefs. The Bass Strait is notorious for its strong currents and unpredictable weather, and the lighthouse's beam, which could be seen for over 30 kilometers, was a welcome sight for weary sailors. Even with advancements in navigation technology, the lighthouse remains a significant aid to navigation, symbolizing the enduring value of traditional maritime safety measures.

Cape Otway Lighthouse is easily accessible from the nearby towns of Apollo Bay and Lorne, located along the scenic Great Ocean Road. This world-famous route provides travelers with stunning coastal views and connects visitors to the lighthouse, which is only a short detour from the main road. The Great Ocean Road itself is a popular attraction, with numerous lookouts, beaches, and natural landmarks that make it a favorite for road trips. Additionally, Melbourne, the nearest major city, is approximately a three-hour drive away, making Cape Otway a feasible day trip for those exploring Victoria's coastline.

As evening falls and Cape Otway Lighthouse shines its light over the Bass Strait, this historic structure continues its watch over the waters, standing as a testament to Australia's maritime history. For over 170 years, it has endured the harsh conditions of the Southern Ocean, guiding ships and inspiring visitors who marvel at its resilience. Cape Otway Lighthouse is more than just a beacon; it is a place of reflection, where history, nature, and human endeavor converge. It serves as a reminder of the courage and dedication of those who built it and those who continue to preserve it, ensuring that its light will continue to shine for generations to come.

17. Cape Reinga Lighthouse - New Zealand

Cape Reinga Lighthouse, standing proudly at the northern tip of New Zealand's North Island, is a beacon of cultural and natural significance. Positioned on a rugged cliff where the Tasman Sea meets the Pacific Ocean, the lighthouse is modest in height yet carries an immense presence in its remote and striking location. Built in 1941, this lighthouse replaced a smaller beacon on nearby Motuopao Island, becoming a critical navigational aid for ships approaching the northern coast of New Zealand. Its sturdy white structure and black lantern room are simple yet iconic, reflecting its role as a protector of the seas and a symbol of the region's spiritual heritage.

Cape Reinga itself holds deep cultural meaning for the Māori people, who believe it to be the departing point for spirits journeying to the afterlife. The name "Reinga" translates to "underworld" in Māori, while "Te Rerenga Wairua," another name for the area, means "the leaping place of spirits." According to Māori legend, spirits make their final journey from Cape Reinga to their ancestral homeland, Hawaiki, creating a sacred and revered atmosphere around the lighthouse. This spiritual connection adds a layer of significance that extends beyond its practical purpose, making it a destination of reflection and respect for visitors.

The climate at Cape Reinga is often mild but influenced by its coastal exposure. Summers are warm, with temperatures averaging around 75°F (24°C), while winters are cooler, averaging around 55°F (13°C). The area is frequently windy, and the cliffs are often shrouded in mist or fog, adding to the mystical aura of the site. The weather can change rapidly, with sudden showers and strong gusts rolling in from the ocean. Despite the unpredictable conditions, the lighthouse stands resilient, a symbol of strength against the forces of nature.

Cape Reinga Lighthouse has become a popular tourist attraction, with thousands of visitors traveling to this remote point to experience the breathtaking scenery and cultural heritage. From the viewing platform near the lighthouse, visitors can see the distinct line where the Tasman Sea and Pacific Ocean meet, their waves crashing and swirling together. This natural phenomenon, combined with the panoramic views of the cliffs and open ocean, creates a powerful and unforgettable experience. The walk to the lighthouse offers a sense of journey and exploration, as visitors make their way to the edge of the land, feeling the full impact of this spiritual place.

The landscape around the lighthouse is dominated by coastal vegetation, with native shrubs, grasses, and flax plants that cling to the cliffs. The area is part of a protected conservation zone, ensuring that the natural beauty and native flora remain undisturbed. The fauna includes seabirds like gannets and gulls, which can be seen gliding over the waves, while occasionally, dolphins and orcas are spotted in the waters below. The Cape Reinga region is a living reminder of New Zealand's biodiversity, offering a glimpse of the unique ecosystems that thrive in this remote part of the world.

For the people of New Zealand, Cape Reinga Lighthouse is more than just a navigational aid; it is a national symbol and a place of deep cultural importance. It embodies the connection between land and

LIGHTHOUSE: BEACON OF HISTORY AND LIGHT

sea, past and present, nature and spirituality. The lighthouse's role in guiding ships safely around the northern coast is matched by its symbolic role as a guiding point in Māori mythology. Its presence has helped shape the identity of the Northland region, drawing people from all over New Zealand and beyond to experience its beauty and significance.

The lighthouse's location on the northernmost tip of New Zealand presents unique challenges. The remote setting makes maintenance difficult, and access can be challenging, especially during bad weather. However, the lighthouse's design is well-suited to its environment, built to withstand the winds and salt air that erode the coastline. Its automation in 1987 has allowed it to continue operating reliably without the need for an on-site keeper, but regular inspections are still necessary to ensure it remains in working order.

A lesser-known fact about Cape Reinga Lighthouse is that it uses a solar-powered light, which was installed during an upgrade in the early 21st century. This eco-friendly approach aligns with New Zealand's commitment to sustainability and adds to the lighthouse's role as a model of resilience and adaptation. The solar light has a range of 19 nautical miles, providing an essential guide for ships despite its remote and challenging location.

Cape Reinga Lighthouse's importance as a navigational aid cannot be overstated. Its light serves as a beacon for ships traveling along the northern coast, helping them avoid the dangers posed by submerged rocks and strong currents. The meeting of two oceans at Cape Reinga creates unique and often hazardous conditions, and the lighthouse's light provides a reassuring presence for mariners navigating these waters. Its strategic location at the tip of New Zealand makes it a crucial part of the country's maritime safety network, contributing to the safe passage of vessels around the North Island.

Traveling to Cape Reinga Lighthouse is a journey in itself. The nearest major town, Kaitaia, is about 100 kilometers south, and from there, visitors can drive along State Highway 1, which leads directly to the cape. The road passes through the scenic landscapes of Northland, including rolling hills, lush forests, and stretches of coastline. For those without a vehicle, bus tours operate from nearby towns, providing an accessible way to reach this iconic destination. The journey is as much a part of the experience as the destination, with the drive offering a sense of the remoteness and beauty of New Zealand's northern reaches.

As night falls and the solar-powered light of Cape Reinga Lighthouse shines across the darkened ocean, the lighthouse becomes a beacon not only for ships but for all who visit. It is a place of history, culture, and natural wonder, where the forces of nature and the spirit of New Zealand come together. For generations, it has stood watch over the seas, embodying the resilience and heritage of the land. Cape Reinga Lighthouse is more than a structure; it is a place of reflection, a bridge between worlds, and a reminder of the enduring beauty of New Zealand's northern coast. For all who visit, it offers a moment of awe and a connection to something greater, a place where land meets sea and the spirit of the land speaks to all who come to listen.

18. Cape Wrath Lighthouse - UK (Scotland)

Cape Wrath Lighthouse, standing resolutely on the cliffs of Scotland's northern coast, is one of the most remote and iconic beacons in the United Kingdom. Built in 1828, this lighthouse rises 20 meters (66 feet) above the rugged terrain, its white stone tower capped by a black lantern, casting its beam over the wild North Atlantic Ocean. Cape Wrath, known for its dramatic cliffs and untamed beauty, marks the northwesternmost point of mainland Scotland. The lighthouse's isolation and stark setting make it a fascinating place, embodying the resilience required to withstand both the fierce elements and the challenges of time.

The construction of Cape Wrath Lighthouse was overseen by the renowned Scottish engineer Robert Stevenson, grandfather of famed writer Robert Louis Stevenson. Built to improve navigation for ships traveling around Scotland's northern coast, the lighthouse was part of a broader effort to safeguard maritime routes. The strong currents, unpredictable weather, and rocky coastline around Cape Wrath posed significant dangers to vessels, and the lighthouse became a critical aid, casting its light 22 nautical miles out to sea. The original light source was a large oil lamp, later upgraded to an electric light, a testament to the continuous advancements in lighthouse technology.

Cape Wrath's climate is shaped by its exposed position on the Atlantic, bringing frequent storms, high winds, and rainfall. Summers are mild, with average temperatures around 55°F (13°C), while winters are cold, often dipping to near freezing. The harsh weather conditions and the constant battering of Atlantic winds have given Cape Wrath an atmosphere of mystery and beauty. Fog is common, particularly in spring and autumn, adding to the lighthouse's isolation, as the mist shrouds the cliffs and ocean, making the lighthouse's guiding beam all the more essential for mariners.

Despite its remote location, Cape Wrath Lighthouse has become a popular destination for adventurous travelers seeking to experience Scotland's wild beauty. The journey to Cape Wrath requires determination; access is limited, and visitors must cross the Kyle of Durness by ferry before taking a rugged 11-mile track to reach the lighthouse. The cliffs surrounding Cape Wrath offer stunning views, and the lighthouse itself stands as a beacon not only for ships but for all who wish to see Scotland's rugged coastline in its rawest form.

The cliffs and moorland around Cape Wrath support a variety of flora and fauna. Coastal plants, including heather, gorse, and wild grasses, thrive in the salty air, adding a splash of color to the otherwise stark landscape. The cliffs are home to colonies of seabirds, such as puffins, guillemots, and kittiwakes, which nest along the rock ledges. The waters below are frequented by seals, dolphins, and, occasionally, whales. This biodiversity adds to the natural allure of Cape Wrath, making it a haven for nature enthusiasts and birdwatchers.

For the people of Scotland, Cape Wrath Lighthouse is not only a navigational aid but also a symbol of resilience and heritage. It represents Scotland's long maritime history and the ingenuity of the

LIGHTHOUSE: BEACON OF HISTORY AND LIGHT

engineers who created it. The lighthouse has become a cultural icon, celebrated for its endurance against the elements and the challenges posed by its remote location. Its presence on the coast has influenced the identity of the Highlands, drawing visitors from across the world to experience the power of nature at the edge of the continent.

Maintaining Cape Wrath Lighthouse is a considerable challenge. The remote location makes transportation of supplies difficult, especially in winter when storms can make access nearly impossible. Despite being automated since the 1990s, the lighthouse requires regular maintenance to withstand the effects of harsh weather. Erosion from the constant exposure to wind and rain has worn down parts of the structure, necessitating repairs to keep it operational. The UK's Northern Lighthouse Board oversees its upkeep, ensuring that this historic landmark remains functional for both safety and heritage.

One lesser-known fact about Cape Wrath Lighthouse is its connection to the Stevenson family, known for producing generations of engineers who built many of Scotland's most famous lighthouses. Robert Stevenson's legacy lives on in the robust design of Cape Wrath Lighthouse, which has withstood nearly two centuries of challenging conditions. The structure's resilience is a testament to the skill and vision of its builders, who recognized the need for a strong, enduring lighthouse to mark this treacherous point.

The lighthouse's importance to maritime safety cannot be overstated. The North Atlantic waters around Cape Wrath are notoriously difficult to navigate, with shifting currents and frequent storms that can drive ships dangerously close to the rocky coastline. Cape Wrath Lighthouse provides a crucial point of reference for vessels, guiding them safely past the cliffs and on toward calmer waters. For generations, its light has been a reassuring presence in the darkness, a symbol of safety and hope for sailors braving the northern seas.

Reaching Cape Wrath Lighthouse is an adventure in itself. The nearest village, Durness, provides access to the Kyle of Durness ferry, which is the first step of the journey. After crossing the Kyle, visitors continue by minibus along a rugged track that traverses the moors and leads to the lighthouse. This journey is part of the appeal, offering a taste of the remoteness and beauty of Scotland's northern coast. The track is impassable for much of the year due to weather conditions, which limits access but also preserves the solitude of this remarkable place.

As the evening draws in and Cape Wrath Lighthouse casts its light over the darkening ocean, it stands as a beacon of endurance and history. For nearly 200 years, it has watched over one of the wildest parts of Scotland, guiding ships and inspiring those who come to witness its beauty. Cape Wrath Lighthouse is more than just a structure; it is a piece of Scottish heritage, a connection to the past, and a symbol of the unyielding spirit required to live and thrive at the edge of the world.

19. Cordouan Lighthouse - France

Cordouan Lighthouse, often called the "King of Lighthouses," stands proudly on a rocky islet at the mouth of the Gironde estuary in France. Built between 1584 and 1611, it is the oldest lighthouse in France still in operation and one of the few that is open to the public. Towering at 67.5 meters, Cordouan is a masterpiece of Renaissance and Classical architecture, with intricate detailing and grand proportions that reflect its historical importance. The lighthouse's beauty and isolation make it a unique marvel, rising from the tidal waters of the Atlantic and standing as a testament to centuries of French maritime heritage.

The idea for Cordouan Lighthouse originated with King Henry III of France, who saw the need for navigational aid to guide ships safely through the dangerous waters of the Gironde estuary. Construction began under his reign and was completed in the early 17th century. Its design was the work of architect Louis de Foix, who envisioned a structure not only as a practical guide for mariners but as a symbol of royal power and sophistication. With a chapel, royal apartments, and richly decorated interiors, Cordouan was unlike any other lighthouse of its time, built to reflect the grandeur of the French monarchy.

Located off the coast near Royan, Cordouan Lighthouse experiences a temperate maritime climate with mild winters and warm summers. Temperatures average around 60°F (15°C) in winter and 75°F (24°C) in summer. The Atlantic winds bring frequent weather changes, and the tidal range can vary dramatically, exposing the rocky base of the lighthouse during low tide and surrounding it with choppy waters at high tide. These conditions add a touch of isolation and mystique, with the lighthouse often appearing as though it is floating on the sea.

Cordouan Lighthouse attracts thousands of visitors each year, who come not only to marvel at its beauty but to explore its rich history. The journey to the lighthouse itself is an adventure, as it can only be reached by boat during low tide. Once on the islet, visitors climb the lighthouse's winding stone staircase to reach the top, where they are rewarded with panoramic views of the Atlantic Ocean and the coast of France. The lighthouse has become a symbol of pride for the region, embodying both architectural grandeur and the endurance of French maritime culture.

The flora and fauna around Cordouan Lighthouse are typical of the Atlantic coast, with hardy coastal plants such as sea lavender and samphire clinging to the rocky surfaces. Seabirds, including gulls and terns, frequent the area, often seen circling the lighthouse or perched on the rocks. The waters around the lighthouse are rich in marine life, including fish and shellfish that thrive in the estuary's unique ecosystem. This biodiversity adds to the lighthouse's allure, creating a vibrant natural setting that complements its historical and cultural significance.

For the people of France, the Cordouan Lighthouse is more than a navigational aid; it is a symbol of the nation's history and architectural legacy. It has been designated a historical monument and was added to the UNESCO World Heritage list in 2021, reflecting its exceptional cultural value. Known as the "Versailles of the Sea," the lighthouse represents a connection to France's royal past, as well as the ingenuity

LIGHTHOUSE: BEACON OF HISTORY AND LIGHT

and dedication required to build and maintain such an isolated structure. Cordouan has become a beloved landmark, cherished not only for its beauty but for the stories it holds within its walls.

The lighthouse's location on a tidal islet poses significant challenges, particularly in terms of maintenance. Constant exposure to salt water, strong winds, and the forces of the Atlantic requires regular upkeep to preserve its structure. In the past, lighthouse keepers faced the difficulties of living in such isolation, enduring harsh weather, and relying on supply deliveries by boat. Today, the lighthouse is automated, but its historical elements are carefully preserved, and maintenance work is essential to protect its intricate carvings, stonework, and other architectural features.

One fascinating fact about Cordouan Lighthouse is its architectural design, which includes a chapel dedicated to Saint Louis, the patron saint of sailors. This chapel, located within the lighthouse, was used by both lighthouse keepers and passing sailors who sought refuge in its walls. The royal apartments, though modest, added a touch of nobility to the structure, emphasizing its dual role as a beacon for mariners and a tribute to the French crown. The combination of utility and luxury makes Cordouan unique among lighthouses, as it was intended not only as a guide but as a monument to French engineering and artistry.

The significance of Cordouan Lighthouse goes beyond its practical function as a beacon. Situated at the meeting point of the Gironde estuary and the Atlantic Ocean, it serves as a gateway to Bordeaux, one of France's major ports. Throughout history, it has guided countless vessels safely into the estuary, protecting them from the hidden dangers of shifting sands and strong currents. Cordouan has thus played an essential role in facilitating trade and communication, symbolizing the importance of France's maritime routes and the safety of those who navigate them.

Reaching Cordouan Lighthouse is a unique experience, with boat tours operating from the nearby towns of Royan and Le Verdon-sur-Mer.

These excursions are carefully timed to coincide with low tide, allowing visitors to disembark on the islet and explore the lighthouse on foot. The boat ride offers views of the French coast and the Gironde estuary, adding to the sense of adventure that accompanies a visit to this remote and remarkable structure. For those willing to make the journey, Cordouan Lighthouse provides an unforgettable glimpse into France's maritime heritage.

As dusk falls and Cordouan Lighthouse illuminates the darkening horizon, its light serves as a reminder of centuries of history and the unwavering dedication of those who have cared for it. The lighthouse stands as a beacon of France's past, its beauty and elegance a testament to the skill and vision of those who built it. Cordouan is more than just a lighthouse; it is a piece of history, a symbol of French pride, and a marvel of architectural achievement. For all who visit, it offers a moment of awe and reflection, a place where history and the sea meet in one of the most enchanting corners of the Atlantic coast.

20. Diamond Head Lighthouse - USA

Diamond Head Lighthouse, perched on the southeastern coast of Oahu, Hawaii, is an iconic landmark with both historical significance and breathtaking beauty. Standing on the slopes of the famous Diamond Head crater, the lighthouse rises 55 feet (17 meters) above the cliff, guiding vessels navigating the Pacific waters off Honolulu. Built in 1899, it serves as a critical navigational aid and a symbol of Hawaiian heritage. The lighthouse's pristine white tower and red-roofed lantern room make it a striking feature against the lush green landscape and the deep blue of the ocean, marking it as one of the most picturesque lighthouses in the United States.

The construction of Diamond Head Lighthouse was spurred by the need to improve maritime safety near Oahu's coast, where hidden reefs and strong currents posed hazards to ships. Originally equipped with a simple oil lamp, the lighthouse has been upgraded over the years with modern technology to maintain its role as an effective guide for ships. Although modest in height compared to some other lighthouses, its elevated position on the cliff gives it an impressive range, allowing its light to be seen for up to 18 miles out to sea. Today, Diamond Head

Lighthouse stands as a blend of functionality and charm, a lighthouse that has witnessed over a century of Hawaiian maritime history.

Located in a tropical climate, Diamond Head experiences warm temperatures year-round, averaging between 75°F (24°C) in winter and 85°F (29°C) in summer. The weather is generally sunny, with occasional trade winds providing a refreshing breeze. However, the area can experience heavy rain showers, particularly in the winter months, adding to the lush greenery that surrounds the lighthouse. This warm, inviting climate contributes to the lighthouse's popularity, as visitors are drawn to the scenic beauty of the coastline and the panoramic views from Diamond Head.

The lighthouse's location near Waikiki Beach and Diamond Head State Monument has made it a popular attraction, with thousands of tourists visiting the area each year. Although the lighthouse itself is not open to the public, its striking appearance against the backdrop of the ocean makes it a favorite for photographers and sightseers. The nearby trails of Diamond Head Crater offer stunning views of the lighthouse and the Honolulu coastline, allowing visitors to experience the area's natural beauty and historical significance in one visit. The lighthouse has become an essential part of the Diamond Head landscape, embodying the spirit of Hawaii and the allure of its coastline.

The flora around Diamond Head Lighthouse includes native Hawaiian plants such as naupaka, kiawe trees, and a variety of tropical flowers that thrive in the warm, humid climate. The area is also home to a variety of bird species, including seabirds like red-footed boobies and frigatebirds, which are often seen soaring over the cliffs and ocean. The lush greenery and vibrant wildlife add to the lighthouse's charm, creating a natural sanctuary that enhances its appeal as both a historical and scenic landmark.

Diamond Head Lighthouse holds a special place in the hearts of Hawaiians. It has become more than a navigational aid; it is a symbol of the Hawaiian spirit and the beauty of the islands. Its presence has

LIGHTHOUSE: BEACON OF HISTORY AND LIGHT

shaped the identity of the area, with locals and visitors alike finding inspiration in its history and its role in safeguarding the coast. For the people of Honolulu, the lighthouse stands as a reminder of Hawaii's maritime heritage, linking the past to the present and serving as a proud emblem of the state's connection to the sea.

Despite its beauty, the location of Diamond Head Lighthouse presents unique challenges. The constant exposure to salt air and ocean winds can cause erosion and wear, requiring regular maintenance to preserve its structure. Additionally, the lighthouse's cliffside position means it is subject to the occasional threat of landslides or earthquakes, adding to the need for careful monitoring and upkeep. However, the United States Coast Guard, which oversees its maintenance, ensures that this historical landmark remains in excellent condition, honoring its past while preparing it for the future.

One interesting fact about Diamond Head Lighthouse is that it has its own distinctive beacon, flashing a white light every 10 seconds. The light is equipped with a Fresnel lens, which enhances its brightness and range, making it visible from great distances. Additionally, the lighthouse serves as the home for the 14th Coast Guard District commander, making it one of the few lighthouses in the United States that serves as an official residence. This unique status adds an extra layer of historical and operational importance, making Diamond Head Lighthouse both a home and a working navigational aid.

The lighthouse's importance extends beyond its immediate location. Positioned on Oahu's southern coast, it guides vessels traveling between the Pacific Ocean and Honolulu Harbor, one of Hawaii's busiest ports. For ships arriving from the mainland United States or Asia, Diamond Head Lighthouse serves as a familiar landmark, signaling their approach to the Hawaiian Islands. Its role in maritime safety has made it an indispensable part of Hawaii's navigational network, ensuring the safe passage of countless vessels over the years.

Visitors to Diamond Head Lighthouse can view it from nearby locations, including the popular Diamond Head Trail, which leads to the summit of the crater and provides a panoramic view of the lighthouse and the surrounding ocean. The area is easily accessible from Honolulu, with public transportation and rental cars providing convenient access for both locals and tourists. The lighthouse's proximity to Waikiki Beach and other famous landmarks makes it a must-see destination for anyone exploring the island of Oahu.

As evening falls and Diamond Head Lighthouse casts its beam over the Pacific, it stands as a symbol of Hawaii's maritime history and the enduring beauty of its coast. For over a century, it has illuminated the waters of Oahu, guiding ships and inspiring those who come to see it. Diamond Head Lighthouse is more than just a navigational tool; it is a part of Hawaii's cultural landscape, a place where history, nature, and human ingenuity meet. For all who visit or see it from afar, the lighthouse remains a beacon of the island's spirit, offering a glimpse into the past and a guide to the future.

21. Dubh Artach Lighthouse - UK (Scotland)

Dubh Artach Lighthouse, standing isolated on a remote islet in the North Atlantic off the coast of Scotland, is one of the most formidable and hauntingly beautiful lighthouses in the United Kingdom. Completed in 1872, this stone tower rises 44 meters (144 feet) from the rocky islet that gives it its name, Dubh Artach, meaning "Black Rock" in Gaelic. The lighthouse's sturdy, dark exterior reflects the harsh conditions it endures, as it is exposed to relentless winds, crashing waves, and often treacherous weather. Built to guide vessels through the dangerous waters of the Hebrides, Dubh Artach has become legendary among lighthouses, a testament to human determination and ingenuity.

The story of Dubh Artach's construction is one of resilience in the face of near-impossible conditions. In the mid-19th century, the waters surrounding the islet were infamous for their danger to ships navigating between Ireland and Scotland. Many vessels had been lost in these rough seas, and the need for a lighthouse became evident. Engineer

David Stevenson, part of Scotland's illustrious Stevenson family of lighthouse builders, took on the formidable task of designing and constructing the lighthouse. Between 1867 and 1872, work crews braved the unpredictable North Atlantic, dealing with storms that could last for days, and established a beacon on the "Black Rock" that would serve as a vital guide for ships.

Situated 18 miles from the nearest land, Dubh Artach Lighthouse experiences a temperate maritime climate, with frequent rain, strong winds, and mist. Winter temperatures rarely drop below freezing but the relentless wind and dampness make the cold feel especially biting. The islet is often lashed by fierce Atlantic storms, and during particularly rough seas, waves have been known to reach heights of over 90 feet, sometimes crashing against the lighthouse itself. These extreme conditions make Dubh Artach one of the most exposed and challenging locations for a lighthouse, its remote position making maintenance and access difficult even in modern times.

The lighthouse, though remote, has fascinated many and is regarded as a wonder of engineering. While the structure itself is not accessible to the public, it draws interest from maritime historians and lighthouse enthusiasts, who admire its design and the endurance required to build it in such a perilous location. Dubh Artach is a testament to Scotland's maritime history and engineering prowess, embodying the spirit of exploration and the determination to provide safe passage through even the most treacherous waters.

Flora and fauna around Dubh Artach are minimal due to the lighthouse's isolated position and harsh environment. The islet supports little vegetation beyond hardy coastal grasses and a few resilient mosses that cling to the rocks. Seabirds, however, are frequent visitors, including species such as fulmars, puffins, and guillemots, which nest on the rocky cliffs of nearby islands and often fly around the lighthouse. The surrounding waters are home to seals and occasionally

LIGHTHOUSE: BEACON OF HISTORY AND LIGHT

dolphins, creating a rare ecosystem that, while sparse, adds a touch of life to the otherwise barren landscape.

For Scotland, Dubh Artach Lighthouse represents a landmark of perseverance and maritime safety. It is part of a long tradition of lighthouse building that has protected Scottish waters for centuries. The lighthouse has become a symbol of resilience, embodying the struggle against the forces of nature that define the rugged Scottish coast. Though few have seen it up close, its story resonates deeply with the Scottish people, reflecting the nation's long relationship with the sea and its commitment to preserving lives through technological innovation.

The lighthouse's location on a tiny, exposed islet poses exceptional challenges, especially for maintenance. The site is accessible only by boat or helicopter, and both approaches are risky due to the surrounding rough seas and frequently adverse weather conditions. Originally, lighthouse keepers had to stay on-site for long periods, often unable to leave due to the weather, which could isolate them for weeks at a time. The transition to automation in 1971 eased some of these challenges, but the lighthouse still requires occasional inspections and repairs, which are conducted by specialized teams who navigate the difficult access conditions.

One lesser-known fact about Dubh Artach Lighthouse is that during its construction, the workers faced such severe weather that they often had to suspend work for weeks. The lighthouse base was constructed from granite quarried on the mainland and shipped out to the islet, a process that required incredible precision and perseverance. At times, the workers lived on the islet in makeshift shelters, enduring storms and the ever-present danger of high waves that could sweep them off the rocks. Their resilience and dedication have become legendary, adding to the mystique of Dubh Artach and highlighting the human spirit's capacity to overcome adversity.

The importance of Dubh Artach Lighthouse is considerable, as it sits in one of Scotland's most dangerous stretches of water. The light from Dubh Artach provides a crucial navigational aid for vessels passing through the area, helping them avoid the submerged reefs and rocky outcrops that have claimed many ships over the centuries. Its powerful beam, visible for over 18 miles, has been a lifeline for countless mariners, ensuring safe passage in waters notorious for their hazards. Despite modern navigation systems, the lighthouse continues to serve as a backup guide, underscoring the timeless value of traditional navigational aids in safeguarding human lives.

Reaching Dubh Artach Lighthouse is no simple task. The nearest village on the mainland, Oban, serves as a starting point for journeys out to the lighthouse, though these trips are typically reserved for maintenance crews or researchers. Boats or helicopters are required for access, with each method posing unique risks due to the challenging weather conditions. The rough seas and strong winds mean that only a select few ever experience Dubh Artach up close, preserving its mystique and reinforcing its reputation as one of the UK's most isolated and awe-inspiring lighthouses.

As the sun sets and Dubh Artach Lighthouse casts its beam across the stormy sea, it stands as a beacon of endurance and human achievement. For nearly 150 years, it has withstood the forces of nature, guiding ships and inspiring all who hear its story. Dubh Artach Lighthouse is more than just a navigational tool; it is a monument to courage, determination, and the unbreakable bond between Scotland and the sea. For all who learn of its legacy, it serves as a reminder of the power of human ingenuity and the timeless beauty of Scotland's rugged coastline.

22. Eddystone Lighthouse - UK

Eddystone Lighthouse, standing alone on a rocky outcrop in the English Channel, is one of the most famous and storied lighthouses in maritime history. Its current structure, the fourth lighthouse built on this treacherous site, is a testament to human resilience and innovation. Rising 49 meters (161 feet) above the rocks, this sturdy stone tower is designed to endure some of the harshest conditions imaginable, withstanding powerful waves, fierce winds, and an isolated, exposed location 14 miles off the coast of Plymouth, England.

The history of Eddystone Lighthouse dates back to the late 17th century when a need for navigational aid became increasingly evident. Ships navigating the busy English Channel frequently met with disaster upon the hidden, jagged rocks of Eddystone Reef. The first lighthouse, constructed by Henry Winstanley in 1698, was an elaborate structure designed to withstand storms; however, it was destroyed in the Great Storm of 1703, taking Winstanley and the keepers with it. The second lighthouse, built by John Rudyard, lasted from 1709 until it burned down in 1755. The third structure, engineered by John Smeaton, was a marvel of engineering and lasted until the foundations eroded. Today's

Eddystone Lighthouse, completed in 1882 by engineer James Douglass, remains one of the UK's most robust and iconic lighthouses, a tribute to centuries of improvement in engineering.

The location of Eddystone Lighthouse subjects it to a severe climate, with temperatures ranging from around 5°C (41°F) in winter to 18°C (64°F) in summer. Winter brings particularly fierce gales and rough seas, with waves often crashing halfway up the tower, making it one of the most challenging places to work or visit. Fog is also frequent in spring and autumn, which can obscure the lighthouse from sight, though its light, flashing twice every ten seconds, remains visible up to 22 nautical miles, a beacon of hope for those at sea.

Eddystone Lighthouse has a legendary status, known far and wide as a symbol of Britain's maritime legacy. While it is not accessible to the public due to its remote location, it draws fascination from maritime historians, engineers, and lighthouse enthusiasts worldwide. The lighthouse has inspired many stories, poems, and paintings over the years, embodying both the peril and allure of the sea. Eddystone's reputation as a feat of human engineering has made it an icon, attracting researchers and storytellers eager to learn about its history and significance.

The rocky outcrop that houses Eddystone Lighthouse is devoid of significant vegetation, as the constant spray of saltwater and battering of waves make plant life nearly impossible. However, the surrounding waters are rich in marine life. Fish, seals, and seabirds, such as seagulls and cormorants, thrive in nutrient-rich currents, creating an ecosystem that is both vibrant and raw. The seabirds often circle the lighthouse, lending an atmospheric quality to the structure as they swoop and soar over the waves.

For the people of the UK, particularly those in the coastal city of Plymouth, Eddystone Lighthouse is a symbol of strength, perseverance, and ingenuity. The light has provided safe passage to generations of sailors, guiding them away from treacherous rocks and ensuring they

LIGHTHOUSE: BEACON OF HISTORY AND LIGHT

reach shore safely. The lighthouse has become part of the region's cultural fabric, a point of pride for Plymouth, and a reminder of the courage of those who built and maintained it. Eddystone stands as a testament to the sacrifices of the lighthouse keepers who braved isolation and dangerous conditions to keep the light shining.

Challenges in maintaining Eddystone Lighthouse have been numerous, given its isolated and exposed location. The structure is accessed only by helicopter or boat, and landing is possible only during calm weather conditions. Over the years, advances in technology have enabled better maintenance and automation, eliminating the need for keepers on-site, but even today, weather conditions can complicate repair efforts. The tower's outer shell is designed to withstand constant exposure to saltwater, but ongoing maintenance is necessary to combat the relentless impact of waves and high winds.

One interesting fact about Eddystone Lighthouse is the engineering legacy of its third structure, designed by John Smeaton in 1759. Smeaton's lighthouse, constructed with interlocking stone blocks, introduced new methods that revolutionized lighthouse construction. His design influenced lighthouses around the world and set the foundation for modern engineering principles. Though the Smeaton lighthouse was eventually replaced, the base remains on the rocks, a historic relic that continues to tell the story of innovation.

Eddystone Lighthouse's importance as a navigational aid cannot be overstated. Positioned in one of the world's busiest maritime routes, it helps prevent ships from running aground on the perilous rocks of Eddystone Reef. The waters around the lighthouse are challenging to navigate, with strong currents and shifting sands that can disorient even experienced mariners. The lighthouse's light, casting its beam far into the distance, is a welcome sight for sailors, providing an indispensable guide through a historically dangerous section of the English Channel.

Access to Eddystone Lighthouse is restricted to maintenance crews and officials, with Plymouth acting as the main logistical hub for these journeys. Helicopters are the most common mode of transport to the lighthouse, especially during winter when sea conditions make boat access difficult. The challenging nature of accessing Eddystone has added to its allure, with few ever having the opportunity to set foot on the outcrop itself, maintaining its aura of mystery and isolation.

As the sun sets and Eddystone Lighthouse shines its powerful beam across the waters, it stands as a beacon of endurance and a witness to centuries of maritime history. For over three hundred years, it has braved the storms and witnessed the evolution of lighthouse engineering, guiding sailors safely through some of the English Channel's most treacherous waters. Eddystone Lighthouse is more than a structure; it is a legacy, a testament to human courage, and a symbol of the unwavering spirit that defines Britain's relationship with the sea. For all who know its story, Eddystone remains a place of inspiration, a beacon that lights the way for those navigating the challenges of the open water.

23. Fanad Head Lighthouse - Ireland

Fanad Head Lighthouse stands majestically on the rugged cliffs of Donegal, Ireland, overlooking the vast expanse of the Atlantic Ocean. Built in 1817, this iconic structure reaches 22 meters (72 feet) in height and stands at the entrance to Lough Swilly, one of Ireland's most scenic inlets. Fanad Head was established after a tragic maritime accident in 1811, when the Royal Navy frigate Saldanha was wrecked off the coast, with no survivors. This disaster highlighted the need for a guiding light to aid vessels navigating the treacherous waters around Donegal, leading to the construction of Fanad Head Lighthouse. Today, it stands not only as a navigational beacon but as a cherished landmark deeply rooted in Ireland's history and culture.

Perched on a narrow headland surrounded by cliffs and dramatic rocky outcrops, Fanad Head Lighthouse's position is both strategic and picturesque. Its white tower and attached keeper's quarters stand in stark contrast to the emerald green grass and the often tumultuous gray-blue of the Atlantic Ocean. The tower's elevation provides visibility for miles, with the light reaching 29 kilometers (about 18 miles) out to sea, ensuring the safety of vessels approaching the Irish coast. The lighthouse was originally lit by a single paraffin lamp, which was later upgraded to electric power, enabling a brighter and more reliable beacon.

The climate at Fanad Head is mild yet heavily influenced by the Atlantic Ocean. Winters are cool, with temperatures averaging around 41°F (5°C), and summers are mild, rarely exceeding 64°F (18°C). The coastal location brings frequent rain and strong winds, especially during winter storms when powerful gusts sweep across the cliffs. This ever-changing weather creates an atmosphere of wild beauty around the lighthouse, with the landscape shifting between clear, sunny skies and misty, windswept scenes. Visitors are often captivated by the sight of the lighthouse standing strong against the elements, embodying the resilience required to endure Ireland's northern coast.

Fanad Head Lighthouse has become one of Ireland's most popular tourist destinations, drawing visitors eager to experience the scenic views and historical charm of the site. The lighthouse offers guided tours, where visitors can climb the winding staircase to the top and enjoy panoramic views of the surrounding landscape. From this vantage point, the cliffs, ocean, and sky come together in a breathtaking display, with Lough Swilly visible to the south and the open Atlantic stretching to the north. For those seeking a unique experience, the lighthouse also offers accommodation in the former keeper's quarters, allowing guests to immerse themselves in the history and beauty of Fanad Head.

The cliffs and hills around Fanad Head are covered in vibrant coastal vegetation, including wildflowers, heather, and grasses that sway in the wind. The area is home to a variety of wildlife, particularly seabirds such as puffins, razorbills, and gulls, which nest along the cliffs and can often be seen diving into the waters below. Occasionally, visitors may spot dolphins or seals swimming near the shore, and in the right season, whales pass by on their migratory route, creating an awe-inspiring sight. This rich biodiversity enhances the natural beauty of Fanad Head, making it a haven for birdwatchers and nature enthusiasts alike.

LIGHTHOUSE: BEACON OF HISTORY AND LIGHT

Fanad Head Lighthouse holds a special place in Irish culture and heritage. It is a symbol of the resilience of the Irish people and a reminder of the country's deep connection to the sea. The lighthouse has become an emblem of Donegal, featured in countless photographs, paintings, and travel guides, representing the rugged beauty of Ireland's Wild Atlantic Way. For locals, it is a source of pride and a cherished landmark, embodying the spirit of Ireland's coastal communities who have relied on the sea for generations.

The location of Fanad Head presents certain challenges, particularly about maintenance. The lighthouse is exposed to strong winds, rain, and salt spray, which contribute to the wear and tear of its structure. Regular upkeep is essential to preserve the lighthouse's appearance and functionality, and teams work diligently to ensure that it remains in excellent condition for both navigation and tourism. The modernization of the light system has reduced the need for constant on-site monitoring, but preserving the historical elements of the lighthouse requires careful planning and effort.

One lesser-known fact about Fanad Head Lighthouse is its role in aiding the Coast Guard during wartime. During World War II, the lighthouse's location made it a strategic point for monitoring naval activity in the North Atlantic. It played a role in the "Donegal Corridor," a strip of neutral Irish airspace that allowed Allied planes to pass through, providing vital support to Britain's war efforts. This historical connection adds depth to the lighthouse's legacy, linking it to a broader narrative of Ireland's role in global history.

The importance of Fanad Head Lighthouse cannot be overstated. It provides a critical navigational aid for vessels entering Lough Swilly and those traveling along the northern coast of Ireland. The waters around Donegal are known for their unpredictable currents and rocky seabed, and the lighthouse's light offers a reliable point of reference for ships in need. Its strategic position has made it an essential part of maritime safety in the region, protecting vessels from potential hazards and ensuring safe passage along one of Ireland's most challenging coastlines.

Fanad Head Lighthouse is easily accessible from nearby towns, with roads connecting it to Letterkenny and Donegal Town. For international travelers, Donegal Airport provides convenient access, with car rentals and guided tours available to reach the lighthouse. The site is part of the Wild Atlantic Way, a famous coastal route that spans Ireland's west coast, making it a popular stop for road trips and scenic tours. Visitors can explore the nearby Fanad Peninsula and experience the local culture, hospitality, and natural beauty that define this part of Ireland.

As the sun sets over Fanad Head and the lighthouse casts its beam across the Atlantic, it stands as a beacon of Ireland's coastal heritage. For over two centuries, it has guided sailors safely through these waters, a silent guardian against the perils of the sea. Fanad Head Lighthouse is more than just a structure; it is a symbol of history, resilience, and the enduring allure of Ireland's coastline. For all who visit, it offers a moment of reflection and awe, a chance to connect with the past and witness the beauty of the land where Ireland meets the sea.

24. Faro de Colón - Dominican Republic

Faro de Colón, or Columbus Lighthouse, stands as a monumental tribute to Christopher Columbus and his legacy in the Dominican Republic. Located in Santo Domingo, this massive concrete structure stretches 210 meters (690 feet) long and 59 meters (193 feet) wide, designed in the shape of a cross. Unlike traditional lighthouses, Faro de Colón is more a symbolic monument than a functional navigational aid. Its construction aimed to honor Columbus's arrival in the Americas and to serve as a cultural landmark, reflecting the deep historical ties between the Dominican Republic and European exploration.

The idea for a monument dedicated to Columbus emerged as early as the 19th century, but it wasn't until 1992, on the 500th anniversary of Columbus's first voyage, that Faro de Colón was finally inaugurated. The project was funded by a combination of national and international contributions, symbolizing the global impact of Columbus's voyages. Designed by Scottish architect J.L. Gleave, the lighthouse includes a mausoleum that purportedly holds Columbus's remains, adding to the intrigue and historical significance of the site. The building's cross shape, visible from the sky, emphasizes its dual role as both a memorial and a symbol of faith.

Santo Domingo, where Faro de Colón is located, enjoys a tropical climate with warm temperatures year-round. The average temperature hovers around 77°F to 86°F (25°C to 30°C). The region experiences a rainy season from May to October, with frequent afternoon showers and occasional tropical storms. The dry season, from November to April, brings more temperate conditions, making this a popular time for visitors. The mild weather enhances the appeal of the lighthouse as a year-round attraction, drawing locals and tourists alike to its expansive grounds and historical exhibits.

Faro de Colón is one of the most visited landmarks in Santo Domingo. Its grandeur and architectural uniqueness make it a popular destination for tourists and a point of pride for locals. The monument's interior houses a museum, which includes exhibits about Columbus's expeditions, artifacts from the colonial era, and displays of the cultural heritage of the Americas. Each evening, a powerful lighting system illuminates the lighthouse in the shape of a cross, visible for miles, creating a powerful visual symbol that reinforces its role as a beacon of history and heritage.

The grounds surrounding the lighthouse feature tropical vegetation, including palm trees and native grasses, giving it an island atmosphere. This natural setting contrasts with the massive concrete structure, emphasizing the blend of cultural and environmental elements that define the Dominican Republic. While the flora around Faro de Colón is limited to landscaped plants and trees, the region's warm climate supports a variety of wildlife, especially birds. Visitors may see hummingbirds, herons, and other tropical species, adding to the area's natural charm.

For the people of the Dominican Republic, Faro de Colón represents a connection to both their history and identity. It serves as a reminder of the country's role in the early days of European exploration and the

LIGHTHOUSE: BEACON OF HISTORY AND LIGHT

profound cultural changes that followed. The monument has sparked discussions on colonial history and the impact of Columbus's arrival in the Americas, providing a space for reflection and education. Schools and cultural organizations frequently organize visits, using the lighthouse as an educational tool to teach about history, identity, and the complexities of Columbus's legacy.

The challenges faced by Faro de Colón are significant, particularly due to its sheer size and the tropical climate. Constant exposure to high humidity, rain, and salt air causes wear and tear on the concrete structure, necessitating ongoing maintenance to preserve its appearance and structural integrity. The upkeep of the lighting system, which illuminates the building in a dramatic cross shape each night, also requires regular attention. Despite these challenges, the Dominican government and heritage organizations work to maintain the monument, recognizing its importance as a national symbol and a prominent tourist attraction.

One fascinating fact about Faro de Colón is the longstanding debate over whether Columbus's remains actually reside there. The remains were allegedly brought to Santo Domingo in the 16th century but were later moved to Seville, Spain. However, in the late 19th century, a box labeled with Columbus's name was discovered in Santo Domingo, leading some to believe that the explorer's remains had never left. Today, Faro de Colón holds what many Dominicans claim are Columbus's authentic remains, adding a layer of mystery and historical intrigue that draws even more visitors.

Faro de Colón's importance extends beyond its role as a historical monument; it is also a place of cultural exchange and education. The museum's exhibits provide insights into the indigenous Taíno culture that existed before Columbus's arrival, as well as the complex colonial history that shaped the Caribbean. Through its displays and events, the lighthouse fosters a dialogue about the region's history, encouraging visitors to reflect on both the positive and negative impacts of European exploration.

The monument's location in Santo Domingo makes it easily accessible for both local residents and international travelers. The nearby Las Américas International Airport connects the Dominican Republic to destinations worldwide, and the city itself is a hub of tourism, drawing visitors with its historic Zona Colonial and beautiful beaches. The Faro de Colón stands as a focal point on these cultural and historical tours, and transportation options like taxis, buses, and rental cars make it convenient for visitors to include in their itineraries.

As evening falls and the lighthouse's illuminated cross shines out over Santo Domingo, Faro de Colón takes on a new dimension as a beacon of remembrance and reflection. It invites contemplation on the legacies of exploration, the blending of cultures, and the transformation of the Americas over centuries. For those who visit, Faro de Colón offers a powerful connection to history, a symbol of both the Dominican Republic's cultural heritage and the broader story of the Americas. As a place of beauty, complexity, and history, it remains a testament to the region's enduring spirit and the lasting impact of its past.

25. Fastnet Rock Lighthouse - Ireland

Fastnet Rock Lighthouse, known as "Ireland's Teardrop," stands alone on a small, rugged outcrop in the North Atlantic Ocean, marking the last piece of Irish land seen by those emigrating to America during the 19th and early 20th centuries. Rising 54 meters (177 feet) above the water, this solitary tower is an iconic symbol of resilience, safeguarding ships passing through some of the most challenging waters off Ireland's coast. Situated 13 kilometers (8 miles) southwest of Cape Clear Island, Fastnet Rock is often exposed to extreme weather, with waves that can crash halfway up the lighthouse tower, emphasizing the immense power of the Atlantic Ocean.

The history of Fastnet Rock Lighthouse is marked by tragedy and perseverance. The first lighthouse, built in 1854, was a cast-iron structure meant to guide ships through the treacherous waters between Ireland and the American continent. However, the original design proved inadequate for the harsh conditions, and by the late 19th century, plans were underway for a more robust structure. The present lighthouse, completed in 1904, was built from massive Cornish granite blocks designed to withstand the ferocity of the sea. Its light, which could be seen up to 27 miles away, became a lifeline for mariners navigating this remote stretch of ocean, offering a beacon of safety in the vast expanse of open water.

The climate around Fastnet Rock is harsh, with frequent storms and powerful winds that sweep across the Atlantic. Winters are cold and tempestuous, with temperatures often hovering just above freezing, while summers bring milder weather but remain cool, with temperatures averaging around 15°C (59°F). The lighthouse is often shrouded in mist or fog, adding to the isolation and creating a hauntingly beautiful atmosphere. This combination of rugged weather and isolation has solidified Fastnet Rock Lighthouse as one of the most challenging locations for lighthouse keepers, who historically braved weeks of solitude, battering waves, and relentless winds.

Today, Fastnet Rock Lighthouse remains a popular site of interest for those fascinated by maritime history and the story of Ireland's coast. Although inaccessible to the general public, boat tours from the mainland provide close-up views of the lighthouse and its dramatic surroundings. Fastnet is also well-known among the sailing community, serving as a key waypoint in the renowned Fastnet Race, one of the most challenging offshore yacht races in the world. This biennial event, which begins on the Isle of Wight, takes sailors around Fastnet Rock before returning to Plymouth, England, making the lighthouse a symbolic marker in the world of competitive sailing.

Due to its location on an isolated rock, Fastnet Rock has limited flora, with only a few hardy grasses and mosses managing to cling to the craggy surface. However, the surrounding waters are rich in marine life, including dolphins, seals, and various seabirds that nest on the nearby cliffs. Species such as gannets, puffins, and fulmars frequent the area, often seen soaring around the lighthouse or diving into the waves below. These seabirds add a touch of life to the otherwise stark environment, creating a unique ecosystem where nature and history converge.

LIGHTHOUSE: BEACON OF HISTORY AND LIGHT

For Ireland, Fastnet Rock Lighthouse is a symbol of endurance and a piece of national heritage. It represents the courage of those who built and maintained it, standing as a reminder of Ireland's deep connection to the sea. The lighthouse has become an iconic image in Irish culture, celebrated in literature, art, and music, and remains a source of pride for the Irish people. Its image is instantly recognizable, symbolizing both Ireland's natural beauty and its maritime legacy.

Maintaining Fastnet Rock Lighthouse has always posed significant challenges. Access to the rock is limited to calm weather conditions, and historically, lighthouse keepers were stationed on Fastnet for weeks at a time, often enduring isolation and severe weather. The structure requires ongoing upkeep to withstand the relentless pounding of waves, which have eroded parts of the rock over time. Since the lighthouse was automated in 1989, the need for permanent staffing has been eliminated, but regular inspections and maintenance are still essential to preserve this historical structure.

One intriguing fact about Fastnet Rock Lighthouse is that it was constructed with an innovative design. The granite blocks were interlocked with great precision to ensure stability and durability, allowing the structure to withstand waves and wind that would otherwise wear down lesser buildings. This engineering feat reflects the skill and vision of its builders, who understood the need for a strong foundation in such an exposed location. This design not only helped the lighthouse survive the harsh elements but also set a standard for lighthouse construction in extreme environments.

The importance of Fastnet Rock Lighthouse cannot be overstated. Positioned on the edge of Europe, it serves as a vital navigational aid for ships crossing the Atlantic, guiding vessels through the dangerous waters off Ireland's southern coast. The lighthouse's light, visible for miles, has helped countless mariners avoid the hazards posed by hidden reefs and powerful currents. In the days before modern navigation systems, Fastnet Rock Lighthouse was an essential beacon for transatlantic travelers, providing reassurance and direction for those embarking on long, perilous journeys.

Access to Fastnet Rock Lighthouse is only possible by boat, typically from Baltimore or Schull on Ireland's southwest coast. Boat tours offer visitors the chance to view the lighthouse up close, though landing on the rock itself is restricted due to the challenging conditions and the protection of the structure. For the Irish diaspora, particularly those with ancestors who emigrated during the 19th century, Fastnet holds a special significance as the last part of Ireland seen before leaving their homeland. The lighthouse has thus become a symbol of departure and farewell, a point of connection between Ireland and the wider world.

As waves crash against the rock and Fastnet Lighthouse casts its beam into the Atlantic, it stands as a testament to human ingenuity and the spirit of exploration. For over a century, it has provided safe passage, marking the boundary between land and the vast ocean beyond. Fastnet Rock Lighthouse is more than just a structure; it is a piece of Ireland's soul, a symbol of resilience, and a guiding light that has witnessed the comings and goings of generations. For all who see it, whether from a boat or in a photograph, Fastnet remains a powerful reminder of Ireland's connection to the sea and the enduring strength of those who navigate its waters.

26. Galle Lighthouse - Sri Lanka

Galle Lighthouse stands gracefully on the southern coast of Sri Lanka, a beacon of history and beauty that has watched over the waves for over a century. Rising elegantly at 26 meters in height, this cylindrical, whitewashed tower is a prominent feature of Galle's coast, visible from various parts of the fort and even from the ocean. Its simplicity, combined with a picturesque setting, captures the essence of Sri Lanka's colonial maritime history. Encircled by tall swaying coconut palms, the lighthouse stands close to the shoreline, where the clear blue waters of the Indian Ocean kiss the land, adding to its allure.

Located within the Galle Fort, a UNESCO World Heritage Site, the lighthouse has become an emblem of the city. Built initially by the British in 1848, it was reconstructed in 1939 following a fire, giving it a renewed life that continues to this day. The fort itself was constructed much earlier by the Portuguese and later expanded by the Dutch, making this area rich in layers of history. The geographical location of the lighthouse is in the southwest part of Sri Lanka, right on the edge of the Indian Ocean, which made it crucial for ancient maritime navigation, especially before the advent of modern technology.

The climate surrounding the lighthouse is typically tropical, with two main monsoon seasons bringing rains between May and September, and again from November to February. During these times, the skies darken, waves become tumultuous, and the lighthouse stands resilient against the strong winds and rains. In the remaining months, the weather is more forgiving, with calm seas and clear blue skies. Temperatures generally range from 25 to 30 degrees Celsius throughout the year, creating a warm, humid environment that nurtures the lush flora surrounding the structure.

The importance of Galle Lighthouse extends far beyond its historical and aesthetic appeal. In its early years, it served as a crucial navigational aid to sailors approaching the tricky coastline. Even today, while advanced navigation technology has taken over, the lighthouse continues to guide small boats and local fishermen, upholding its legacy of service. Its light, which flashes every few seconds, is a comforting sight for those at sea, a reminder of land nearby.

The area surrounding Galle Lighthouse is teeming with natural beauty. The flora includes a variety of tropical plants and palm trees, which thrive in the humid climate and contribute to the picturesque landscape. Coconut trees tower above, their leaves rustling in the coastal breeze, while smaller plants and shrubs add a layer of green around the base. The fauna, while not directly influenced by the lighthouse, includes seabirds that are often seen flying around the fort area, occasionally perching near the lighthouse itself. These birds, along with butterflies that flutter around the plants, add life to the environment, creating a harmonious scene where nature and history coexist.

Socially, the lighthouse holds a special place in the hearts of locals and visitors alike. It has become a gathering spot within the fort, where people come to enjoy the sunset, capture photographs, or simply relax by the sea. Over time, it has become a popular destination for tourists, enhancing the local economy by attracting people to nearby businesses

LIGHTHOUSE: BEACON OF HISTORY AND LIGHT

and cafes. Its towering presence against the evening sky has made it a beloved symbol for the city of Galle, creating a shared sense of pride among the locals.

Despite its appeal, Galle Lighthouse faces challenges common to coastal structures. The harsh saltwater environment leads to erosion, while the constant exposure to strong winds and rains during the monsoon seasons accelerates wear and tear. Maintenance efforts are regularly undertaken to preserve the structure, ensuring that it remains standing strong for future generations. However, with climate change and rising sea levels, there are growing concerns about the long-term impact on the surrounding area, which might lead to further complications in preserving this historic monument.

One of the lesser-known facts about Galle Lighthouse is that it is the oldest light station in Sri Lanka. Although the original structure no longer stands, the site itself has continued to serve as a guiding light for seafarers for over 150 years. Another interesting aspect is that the lighthouse is positioned within the fort rather than directly on the shore, which is unusual for most coastal lighthouses. This placement gives it added protection from the ocean while offering a scenic view of both the land and sea.

Its strategic location made it vital for colonial powers to control the spice trade routes in the Indian Ocean. Galle, with its well-protected harbor and close proximity to India, became a bustling hub for trade, and the lighthouse was instrumental in ensuring the safe arrival of ships. This historical importance has only deepened with time, as the lighthouse remains a key point of interest for maritime historians and enthusiasts who visit Galle Fort.

Transportation to the lighthouse is readily available, with various modes connecting Galle to major parts of Sri Lanka and beyond. Galle is accessible by road, rail, and sea, with buses and trains running frequently from Colombo, the capital city, which is about 120 kilometers away. Galle Railway Station is connected to the Southern

Rail Line, making it convenient for tourists to visit the fort and lighthouse. With the development of the Southern Expressway, travel time has been significantly reduced, making it easier for locals and tourists to reach this coastal gem. Additionally, the Galle Port continues to serve small vessels, keeping the maritime spirit of the city alive.

Galle Lighthouse serves as more than a navigational aid or a tourist attraction; it embodies the resilience of the people and the historical significance of the city. Through years of colonial rule, natural disasters, and changing times, it has remained steadfast, watching over the city and the ocean, a silent guardian with tales to tell. Visitors who come to see this lighthouse often find themselves swept up not only by its beauty but also by the sense of timelessness that it radiates. It stands as a reminder of the past while continuing to play an active role in the present, a true icon of Galle and a testament to Sri Lanka's rich heritage.

27. Gay Head Lighthouse - USA

Perched atop the striking cliffs of Martha's Vineyard, the Gay Head Lighthouse stands as a resilient and historic symbol on the westernmost tip of the island. Towering at around 51 feet, this red-bricked, cylindrical structure has weathered storms, witnessed historical events, and guided countless mariners safely through the treacherous waters surrounding the island. Built in 1856, the lighthouse replaced an earlier wooden structure that had suffered from decay due to exposure to harsh coastal weather. Its current form, a robust brick tower crowned with a black lantern room, has withstood the elements for over a century and a half, serving as a steadfast beacon against the vast expanse of the Atlantic Ocean.

Gay Head Lighthouse is located on a scenic promontory known as the Aquinnah Cliffs, a geological marvel that features vibrant layers of red, orange, brown, and gray clay. This stunning location, with its multicolored cliffs descending sharply into the ocean, offers a striking contrast to the deep blues of the surrounding waters. The cliffs themselves hold sacred significance for the Wampanoag Tribe, the native people of the island, who have long regarded this site as a place of spiritual and cultural importance. The lighthouse, standing near this sacred ground, adds a layer of history and human ingenuity to the natural beauty of the cliffs.

Martha's Vineyard experiences a temperate maritime climate, with warm summers and relatively mild winters compared to the mainland. Average temperatures range from around 24°C (75°F) in summer to 0°C (32°F) in winter. The ocean breeze moderates the climate, keeping the summers pleasant and the winters bearable. However, the lighthouse often faces harsh winds, especially during the winter months when storms frequently roll in from the Atlantic. These winds and the corrosive salt air present constant challenges to the maintenance of the lighthouse, which has undergone various restorations over the years to preserve its structural integrity.

Popular among tourists, historians, and photographers, Gay Head Lighthouse draws visitors who are captivated by its scenic location and historical importance. It is one of the most frequently photographed sites on Martha's Vineyard, offering breathtaking views of the cliffs, the ocean, and, on clear days, even the mainland. The lighthouse also serves as a critical navigational aid for ships passing through the surrounding waters. Its light, visible from a distance of over 16 miles, has been a guiding star for generations of sailors navigating the unpredictable waters of Vineyard Sound and the Atlantic.

The surrounding area boasts a variety of native flora, with grasses, wildflowers, and coastal shrubs creating a lush green carpet on the cliffs. In spring and summer, the landscape is dotted with blooming wildflowers, adding vibrant colors to the already picturesque scenery. Wildlife is also plentiful; seabirds such as seagulls and ospreys frequent the area, and it's not uncommon to spot seals along the coastline. The ecosystem around the lighthouse thrives despite the strong winds and salt spray, creating a rugged yet beautiful environment that adds to the charm of the site.

LIGHTHOUSE: BEACON OF HISTORY AND LIGHT

Socially, Gay Head Lighthouse has played a significant role in the local community. It has been a point of pride for the island's residents and a symbol of resilience for the Wampanoag Tribe, who have a deep connection to the Aquinnah Cliffs. In 2015, due to increasing concerns about coastal erosion, the lighthouse faced the threat of collapse. This looming danger sparked a massive community effort to save the structure. The "Save the Gay Head Lighthouse" campaign successfully raised funds to relocate the lighthouse approximately 135 feet inland, away from the rapidly eroding cliffs. This monumental move preserved the lighthouse for future generations and highlighted the community's dedication to safeguarding its heritage.

One of the lesser-known challenges faced by the lighthouse is the constant battle against erosion. The cliffs, composed primarily of clay, are highly susceptible to erosion from wind and water. Over the years, storms and rising sea levels have gradually eaten away at the cliffside, bringing the lighthouse perilously close to the edge. The 2015 relocation was a testament to modern engineering and community spirit, ensuring that the lighthouse remained a fixture of Martha's Vineyard's landscape.

Few realize that the Gay Head Lighthouse has the distinction of being one of the first lighthouses in the United States to be outfitted with a Fresnel lens in the mid-19th century. This innovation greatly improved the visibility and effectiveness of the lighthouse, making it a model for other lighthouses across the country. The original Fresnel lens, however, was removed and replaced with modern lighting technology as the lighthouse evolved to meet contemporary needs. The lens itself, a piece of maritime history, is preserved and displayed at the Martha's Vineyard Museum, serving as a link to the lighthouse's storied past.

The significance of Gay Head Lighthouse extends beyond its role as a navigational aid. As one of the earliest lighthouses established in the U.S., it represents an era when maritime navigation relied heavily on such beacons. The location of the lighthouse is strategic; Vineyard

Sound is one of the busiest shipping routes on the eastern seaboard, and the lighthouse has helped prevent numerous shipwrecks along this stretch. Its steadfast light has saved countless lives, making it an invaluable part of American maritime history.

Transportation to Martha's Vineyard is well-facilitated, with ferries running regularly from the mainland. Ferries from Woods Hole, Massachusetts, provide easy access to the island for both locals and tourists. Additionally, Martha's Vineyard has a small airport that connects it to other parts of New England and beyond. Visitors to the lighthouse can reach the site by car, bike, or local shuttles that run throughout the island, making it an accessible destination for those eager to witness its beauty.

As Gay Head Lighthouse continues to stand watch over the cliffs and waters of Martha's Vineyard, it remains a symbol of resilience, adaptation, and community pride. For those who visit, it offers a glimpse into the island's history, a chance to experience the dramatic natural beauty of the cliffs, and the opportunity to connect with the spirit of a place that has long served as a guiding light, both literally and figuratively. The lighthouse's legacy is not just in the light it shines but in the hearts of the people who have worked tirelessly to preserve it, ensuring that this historic structure continues to inspire and protect for generations to come.

28. Great Basses Reef Lighthouse - Sri Lanka

The Great Basses Reef Lighthouse stands tall in the open waters of the Indian Ocean, a solitary guardian positioned on a reef about ten kilometers off the southern coast of Sri Lanka. Rising to a height of approximately 34 meters, this cylindrical structure, painted in red and white, is perched atop a rocky outcrop, surrounded by vibrant turquoise waters. Constructed on a platform to withstand the relentless waves that crash against its base, the lighthouse remains a striking sight against the vast seascape. Its isolated presence, far removed from the mainland, is both a marvel of engineering and a testament to human tenacity, guiding mariners safely through these dangerous waters.

Built in 1873 during the British colonial period, the lighthouse replaced an earlier attempt to mark the treacherous reefs surrounding it. The structure was designed by James Douglass, a prominent lighthouse engineer of the time, and constructed by local laborers who faced harsh conditions while working in the open ocean. Transporting materials, dealing with unpredictable weather, and enduring the relentless waves made this an engineering feat of its time. Today, the Great Basses Reef Lighthouse stands as a remnant of colonial influence, a silent witness to centuries of maritime history.

The lighthouse is situated in an area known for its warm, tropical climate, with temperatures averaging between 26 and 30 degrees Celsius throughout the year. The region experiences two monsoon seasons, from May to September and from November to February, bringing heavy rains and turbulent seas. These monsoons often cause waves to surge over the reef, creating a daunting spectacle around the lighthouse. During calmer months, however, the waters are clearer and calmer, offering a serene view of the coral reef below, which attracts divers and explorers fascinated by the underwater beauty of this isolated site.

While it may not be a tourist hotspot due to its remote location, the Great Basses Reef Lighthouse holds immense significance for navigators and divers. The lighthouse continues to be an essential aid for ships navigating the southern coast of Sri Lanka, warning them of the shallow waters and hidden reefs that could otherwise lead to disaster. The reefs themselves are famed among divers for their rich marine biodiversity, and many adventurous divers make their way to the area to explore the abundant coral formations, vibrant fish species, and even remnants of ancient shipwrecks scattered on the ocean floor. This underwater paradise draws those with a passion for marine life, giving the lighthouse an indirect yet vital role in promoting the conservation of the surrounding reef.

The flora and fauna around the Great Basses Reef are unique, with an abundance of corals, sea anemones, and various fish species thriving in the area. Beneath the waves, the reef is home to colorful coral gardens that provide shelter for an array of marine life, including angelfish, parrotfish, and reef sharks. Sea turtles are also occasionally spotted here, swimming gracefully through the clear waters. While the lighthouse itself is devoid of vegetation due to its harsh environment,

LIGHTHOUSE: BEACON OF HISTORY AND LIGHT

the reef below it teems with life, creating an ecosystem that is both beautiful and fragile.

The Great Basses Reef Lighthouse holds a special place in the local community and among maritime enthusiasts. Its presence on the reef has long been a symbol of safety and resilience, and despite the modern advancements in navigation technology, the lighthouse still functions as a guiding light for smaller vessels and local fishermen. For the people of the nearby coastal towns, it represents a historical landmark and a connection to their maritime heritage. In recent years, there has been a growing interest in the lighthouse's preservation, with local authorities and heritage groups working to maintain the structure and honor its significance.

Despite its importance, the Great Basses Reef Lighthouse faces numerous challenges. Its exposed location makes it vulnerable to the powerful waves and strong winds that batter it throughout the year. The corrosive saltwater accelerates the wear on the structure, necessitating regular maintenance, which is both difficult and costly due to the lighthouse's isolation. Additionally, climate change and rising sea levels pose a long-term threat to the stability of the reef, potentially endangering the lighthouse's foundation. Efforts to preserve the lighthouse are ongoing, but the cost and logistical difficulties of operating in such a remote area remain significant obstacles.

One lesser-known fact about the Great Basses Reef Lighthouse is its role in a fascinating historical incident. In the early 1960s, two British divers, Arthur C. Clarke and Mike Wilson, discovered a treasure trove of silver coins in a wreck near the lighthouse. The coins, believed to be from a 17th-century wrecked ship, sparked interest in the area's history and brought the lighthouse into the spotlight. Clarke, renowned for his work as a science fiction writer, detailed the treasure hunt in his book "The Treasure of the Great Reef," adding an air of mystery and adventure to the lighthouse's already storied history.

The significance of the Great Basses Reef Lighthouse extends beyond its function as a navigational aid. Situated in one of the busiest shipping lanes in the region, it serves as a reminder of the hazards that these waters have posed to mariners for centuries. The area around the lighthouse has seen numerous shipwrecks over the years, and the structure itself was built to prevent further tragedies. For seafarers, its light has been a beacon of hope and safety, and for the coastal communities, it has been a symbol of resilience in the face of nature's challenges.

Access to the lighthouse is limited due to its location far from the mainland. The only way to reach it is by boat, typically from the nearby town of Kirinda. Boats can be chartered to visit the lighthouse, but due to the rough seas and strong currents, the journey can be treacherous, especially during the monsoon seasons. This isolation adds to the allure of the lighthouse, making it a destination for only the most adventurous of explorers. Despite its remote setting, the Great Basses Reef Lighthouse remains connected to the world through the boats that pass by on their way to other destinations, linking this isolated outpost to the broader maritime network.

The Great Basses Reef Lighthouse stands as a testament to human ingenuity, a silent sentinel on the edge of the Indian Ocean. Its enduring presence on the reef is a reminder of the importance of maritime safety and the efforts taken to protect sailors from the dangers of the sea. For those who visit, it offers a rare glimpse into a world where history, nature, and adventure converge, creating a unique experience that leaves a lasting impression. The lighthouse's legacy lives on, not only in the light it casts across the waters but also in the stories it inspires, embodying the spirit of exploration and resilience that defines Sri Lanka's maritime heritage.

29. Green Point Lighthouse - South Africa

Standing proudly along the Cape Town coast, the Green Point Lighthouse is one of South Africa's most iconic navigational landmarks. With its bold red and white stripes, this lighthouse is both functional and visually striking, drawing the eye of visitors and locals alike. Erected in 1824, it is the oldest lighthouse in the country, designed to guide sailors safely around the treacherous waters of the Cape Peninsula, where strong currents and rocky shores posed significant threats to early mariners. The lighthouse rises from a square base, transitioning into a cylindrical structure that reaches 20 meters into the sky. From the top, a powerful beam of light stretches out across the sea, visible from nearly 25 nautical miles, a reassuring sight for sailors navigating the busy waters near the Cape of Good Hope.

Positioned along Cape Town's Atlantic seaboard, the Green Point Lighthouse stands in a vibrant, bustling area known as Mouille Point. Located at the northern end of Green Point, it serves as a boundary marker for the western edge of Cape Town's city center, offering a view of both the cityscape and the expansive Atlantic Ocean. This location is part of a famous scenic route, with the lighthouse surrounded by a landscape that includes a blend of grassy areas, native coastal plants, and rocky shores. The salty breeze and the rhythmic sound of waves crashing against the shore give the area a unique atmosphere, attracting visitors year-round.

Cape Town enjoys a Mediterranean climate, characterized by warm, dry summers and mild, wet winters. From November to February, temperatures often reach highs of around 25 to 30 degrees Celsius, making the area particularly popular among tourists. Winters, from June to August, are cooler with average highs of 15 to 18 degrees Celsius, accompanied by rainfall and occasional storms. Despite the harsher winter weather, the lighthouse stands strong, its light cutting through misty, rain-filled skies to guide vessels safely.

The Green Point Lighthouse is a beloved landmark and a significant tourist attraction. It not only serves as a navigational aid but has also become a popular photo spot and a point of historical interest for visitors exploring Cape Town's coastal area. The lighthouse's unique red and white stripes make it instantly recognizable, and it frequently appears in Cape Town postcards and travel brochures. Its popularity has only grown over the years, drawing visitors who are eager to learn about its history and take in the beautiful coastal views.

Though the Green Point Lighthouse is situated in an urban area, it is still surrounded by diverse flora and fauna. Coastal grasses, wildflowers, and low-growing shrubs thrive in the sandy soil around the lighthouse, providing a touch of greenery amidst the rocky shore. The area is home to various seabirds, such as seagulls and cormorants, which can often be seen perched on rocks or flying around the lighthouse, adding life to the coastal scene. On rare occasions, dolphins and seals can be spotted in the nearby waters, especially during the summer months, further enhancing the experience for those lucky enough to catch a glimpse of the local marine wildlife.

The lighthouse has played a meaningful role in Cape Town's social and historical landscape. As the first lighthouse built in South Africa,

LIGHTHOUSE: BEACON OF HISTORY AND LIGHT

it has become a symbol of the city's maritime heritage. For centuries, it has been a beacon of safety and reassurance for sailors traversing the challenging waters of the Cape Coast. Its establishment marked an important step in improving maritime safety in the region, as shipwrecks were common along the rugged coastline before the lighthouse's construction. Today, it stands as a proud testament to Cape Town's rich maritime history, bridging the past with the present.

However, maintaining the Green Point Lighthouse has not been without challenges. As with any coastal structure, it faces constant wear from the salty air and strong winds, which accelerate corrosion. The lighthouse has undergone several renovations and upgrades over the years to ensure its continued operation. In addition to battling the natural elements, the lighthouse has faced urban development pressures, with increasing numbers of buildings and infrastructure projects emerging around it. Despite these challenges, the lighthouse remains well-maintained and continues to fulfill its role as a crucial navigational aid.

One of the lesser-known facts about the Green Point Lighthouse is that it was once powered by an oil lamp before being upgraded to an electric light in the early 20th century. The original oil lamp, which required constant monitoring and maintenance, was an essential part of the lighthouse's early operations. The transition to electric power marked a significant advancement in the lighthouse's technology, enabling it to shine brighter and more reliably than before. Today, the lighthouse is equipped with modern lighting technology, though the historical charm of its architecture and design has been carefully preserved.

The Green Point Lighthouse holds great importance, not just for its navigational function but also as a cultural and historical asset. Its light has guided countless ships safely around Cape Town's coastline, preventing shipwrecks and saving lives. Located near one of the busiest trade routes in the world, the lighthouse plays a vital role in keeping Cape Town's port area safe for the numerous vessels that pass by each year. Its significance as a historical structure adds to its value, with locals and visitors alike appreciating its role in the development of the city's maritime infrastructure.

Cape Town's accessibility from around the world makes the Green Point Lighthouse a popular spot for international visitors. Cape Town International Airport connects the city to major global destinations, while the port area nearby welcomes numerous cruise ships and cargo vessels. Within the city, tourists can easily reach the lighthouse by car, bus, or even on foot, as it is located near popular attractions like the V&A Waterfront and Sea Point Promenade. The scenic drive along the Atlantic coast offers breathtaking views, making the journey to the lighthouse an experience in itself.

Green Point Lighthouse remains an enduring symbol of Cape Town's maritime legacy. Its powerful light, cutting through the darkness, has provided safety and guidance for generations of sailors. It stands as a reminder of the region's history, its challenges, and its connection to the sea. For those who visit, it offers not only a glimpse into the past but also a chance to witness the resilience of a structure that has withstood time, weather, and change. The lighthouse continues to inspire awe and admiration, ensuring that its legacy will be cherished for years to come.

30. Heraklion Lighthouse - Greece

The Heraklion Lighthouse stands on the historic Venetian harbor in Crete, Greece, a symbol of the island's long-standing connection to the sea and its storied past. Built by the Venetians in the 16th century, this lighthouse is one of the oldest in the region, serving as a beacon for sailors and traders who have navigated the waters of the Mediterranean for centuries. Its structure, a sturdy stone tower rising to a height of about 26 meters, has witnessed the changing tides of history, from the height of Venetian rule to the waves of modern tourism. The lighthouse is cylindrical with an open lantern room at the top, giving it a unique architectural style that reflects the blend of Greek and Venetian influences. Positioned on a stone pier stretching into the Aegean Sea, it serves as both a historical monument and a functional guide for boats entering Heraklion's port.

Heraklion, the capital of Crete, is nestled along Greece's largest island, positioned near the eastern part of the Mediterranean. The city experiences a Mediterranean climate, with hot, dry summers and mild, wet winters. In summer, temperatures can reach up to 30 degrees Celsius, with a bright, sunlit sky that seems to embrace the entire island. Winter, on the other hand, is milder, with temperatures rarely falling below 10 degrees Celsius. This coastal climate is perfect for visitors, who flock to Crete year-round, drawn by the island's beauty, culture, and history. The lighthouse, standing resiliently against the coastal winds, is a reminder of the city's enduring relationship with the sea.

Heraklion Lighthouse is more than just a navigational aid; it is a beloved landmark for locals and tourists alike. The harbor is one of the busiest in Crete, bustling with ferries, fishing boats, and yachts, and the lighthouse serves as a welcoming sight for those arriving by sea. For visitors exploring Heraklion's waterfront, the lighthouse offers a captivating view, especially during sunset, when the sky takes on hues of pink, orange, and purple, creating a magical backdrop that highlights the lighthouse's stone structure. It's a popular spot for photographs and has become a symbol of the city's rich heritage and natural beauty.

The area surrounding the lighthouse is adorned with Mediterranean flora, including small shrubs, wildflowers, and grasses that add a touch of green to the ancient stone walls. Seabirds, particularly gulls, are a common sight around the harbor, circling above and perching on the lighthouse itself. The lighthouse and harbor area offer a tranquil ecosystem, where the interaction between humans and nature is harmonious. The waters surrounding the lighthouse are home to various marine life, from small fish darting among the rocks to dolphins that occasionally make an appearance, adding to the charm and life of the harbor.

For the people of Heraklion, the lighthouse is not only a historical relic but also a cherished part of their cultural identity. It represents a link to the past, a reminder of the Venetian influence that shaped the island's architecture and maritime traditions. Over time, the lighthouse has become a popular gathering spot, where locals stroll along the harbor walls, fish along the pier, or simply enjoy the view. Its presence fosters a sense of pride and connection to the island's history, as generations

LIGHTHOUSE: BEACON OF HISTORY AND LIGHT

of Heraklion residents have grown up with this lighthouse as a familiar sight.

However, maintaining the Heraklion Lighthouse has not been without challenges. Its exposed location on the harbor wall makes it susceptible to harsh sea weather, especially during winter storms when strong winds and high waves batter the coast. Saltwater exposure accelerates erosion, which has necessitated several restoration efforts over the years. The lighthouse's age and historical importance also add complexity to the maintenance process, as preserving its original structure is essential to retaining its historical authenticity. Despite these challenges, local authorities and heritage organizations continue to ensure the lighthouse remains in good condition, preserving it for future generations.

One interesting fact about the Heraklion Lighthouse is that it was originally part of a larger defensive structure built by the Venetians. The Venetians fortified the harbor with walls and towers to protect the city from pirate attacks and invasions, and the lighthouse was constructed as a part of these defenses. Its light was initially produced by an oil lamp, which required daily tending by keepers who climbed the narrow staircase to the top. Over time, the lighthouse underwent modernization, eventually transitioning to electricity, which greatly enhanced its effectiveness as a navigational aid.

The significance of Heraklion Lighthouse extends beyond its function as a beacon for ships; it stands as a testament to Crete's strategic importance in the Mediterranean. Throughout history, the island has been a crossroads for various civilizations, from the Minoans to the Byzantines, Venetians, and Ottomans. Each of these cultures left its mark on Crete, contributing to its rich and diverse heritage. The lighthouse, positioned at the entrance of one of the island's main ports, embodies this history, serving as a silent witness to the passage of countless vessels and the flow of trade and ideas between East and West.

Heraklion is well-connected by sea, with ferries linking the city to other Greek islands and the mainland. The harbor sees regular ferry routes to Athens, Santorini, and Mykonos, making it a vital hub for both residents and tourists. Cruise ships also frequently dock in Heraklion, bringing visitors from around the world who are eager to explore Crete's archaeological sites, beaches, and vibrant culture. The lighthouse, visible from the harbor, is one of the first sights to greet passengers as they arrive, standing as a welcoming symbol of Crete's hospitality.

As the sun sets on the harbor, the Heraklion Lighthouse stands illuminated, casting its light across the calm waters, a beacon of both safety and history. For those who visit, it offers a glimpse into the island's past, a connection to the seafarers who once relied on its light to guide them safely to shore. Its presence on the harbor wall is a reminder of the resilience and timeless beauty of Crete, capturing the essence of an island that has long been at the heart of the Mediterranean. The Heraklion Lighthouse endures, a steadfast symbol of Heraklion's legacy, a bridge between past and present, and a testament to the enduring allure of the Greek coast.

31. Hook Lighthouse - Ireland

Hook Lighthouse stands as a guardian on the rugged Hook Peninsula in County Wexford, Ireland, a sentinel of history and maritime guidance. Towering at 35 meters, this black-and-white-striped lighthouse is one of the oldest operating lighthouses in the world, with a legacy spanning over 800 years. Built in the early 13th century by the monks of the nearby monastery, it was intended to guide sailors safely around the treacherous coastline. The lighthouse's construction is attributed to William Marshal, the Earl of Pembroke, who commissioned the monks to build a beacon to prevent shipwrecks along the perilous shore. Its thick walls, which are nearly four meters wide at the base, are a testament to medieval engineering and have withstood centuries of Atlantic storms and the relentless sea winds.

The Hook Peninsula juts out into the Celtic Sea on Ireland's southeastern coast, where the waters can be unpredictable and wild. Known for its rocky coastline and strong tides, this region has long posed challenges to sailors, making the lighthouse a crucial guide. The lighthouse's location offers breathtaking views of the sea and the surrounding Irish landscape, but its position on the cliff edge means it faces the full brunt of the elements. During winter, when storms rage, waves crash fiercely against the rocks below, while in summer, the view is serene, with the vast blue expanse of the sea meeting the clear sky.

The climate on Hook Peninsula is typically Irish – mild, wet, and unpredictable. Winters are cool, with temperatures ranging from 4 to 8 degrees Celsius, often accompanied by strong winds and rain. Summers are mild, with temperatures hovering around 15 to 20 degrees Celsius, but the sea breeze keeps the air fresh and cool. Misty mornings and frequent rains add a mystical quality to the peninsula, enhancing the lighthouse's timeless and atmospheric presence. The unpredictable weather has only added to the allure of the lighthouse, which seems almost otherworldly as it emerges from the mist or stands tall against stormy skies.

Over the centuries, Hook Lighthouse has become an iconic landmark and a popular tourist destination. It draws thousands of visitors each year who are fascinated by its history, architecture, and the stunning coastal landscape surrounding it. The lighthouse is open to the public, offering guided tours that allow visitors to ascend the ancient winding stairs to the lantern room, where panoramic views of the peninsula and the Celtic Sea await. The nearby visitor center provides historical insights and amenities, making it a must-visit destination for travelers exploring Ireland's ancient structures and natural beauty.

The landscape around the lighthouse is marked by rugged coastal flora, with grasses and wildflowers clinging to the rocky ground. Seabirds, such as puffins, gulls, and gannets, are a frequent sight, nesting in the cliffs and diving into the sea for fish. Occasionally, seals can be spotted resting on the rocks or swimming near the shore, while dolphins are known to play in the waters off the coast. The area is rich in biodiversity, with marine and coastal ecosystems thriving in the challenging environment. The lighthouse stands amidst this natural setting, a silent witness to the cycles of life around it.

LIGHTHOUSE: BEACON OF HISTORY AND LIGHT

Locals hold a deep sense of pride in Hook Lighthouse, viewing it as a symbol of resilience and continuity. The lighthouse has been a part of the community's life for centuries, with generations of lighthouse keepers having maintained the beacon before automation took over. It has seen changes in technology, from wood and coal fires to oil lamps, and finally, to modern electric lights. For the people of the Hook Peninsula, the lighthouse represents a link to their maritime heritage, a constant presence that has outlived wars, storms, and the passage of time.

Maintaining such an ancient structure presents its own set of challenges. The salty sea air accelerates corrosion, while the wind and rain take their toll on the masonry. Over the years, restoration efforts have been necessary to preserve the lighthouse. Local and national heritage organizations have worked tirelessly to ensure its survival, implementing modern preservation techniques while respecting its historical integrity. Additionally, the lighthouse's isolated location on the peninsula adds logistical challenges, as materials and workers must navigate narrow roads to reach the site. However, these challenges have not deterred efforts to keep the lighthouse standing, as it remains a cherished landmark.

One fascinating fact about Hook Lighthouse is its continuous operation for over 800 years, making it one of the oldest operational lighthouses in the world. Legend has it that the monks who built the lighthouse would light fires on the top to guide sailors, making it one of the earliest forms of navigational aid. The design itself, with thick walls and a simple yet robust structure, has allowed it to withstand the test of time. The lighthouse has also inspired local folklore, with stories of ghostly apparitions and mysterious lights adding to its mystique.

The significance of Hook Lighthouse lies not only in its function but also in its cultural and historical importance. As one of Ireland's most enduring symbols, it represents the country's maritime legacy, a reminder of the bravery and skill of sailors who once navigated these challenging waters. Positioned near a strategic point on the southeastern coast, the lighthouse has been crucial in ensuring safe passage for ships entering the Irish Sea, a role that it continues to play in the present day. Its longevity and resilience are emblematic of Ireland's own spirit, blending history, myth, and natural beauty.

Access to Hook Lighthouse is relatively straightforward, with well-maintained roads connecting the peninsula to nearby towns and cities. Visitors can drive from Dublin, which is about two hours away, or take local transport options from Waterford, the nearest city. Hook Peninsula is a popular stop on Ireland's Ancient East tourist trail, which promotes historical sites and scenic spots along Ireland's eastern coast. While the lighthouse's isolated setting gives it a sense of remoteness, its accessibility makes it a favorite destination for both locals and international tourists.

Today, Hook Lighthouse stands as a symbol of Ireland's rich history and natural beauty, a beacon of hope and guidance for generations past and present. Its light continues to shine over the waters of the Celtic Sea, a timeless reminder of the island's connection to the ocean. For those who visit, the lighthouse offers a unique experience, combining breathtaking views, historical insights, and a sense of peace that only comes from standing at the edge of the world. Hook Lighthouse is more than just a navigational aid; it is a piece of Ireland's soul, an enduring testament to human ingenuity and the power of tradition.

32. Jeddah Light - Saudi Arabia

Jeddah Light stands as a beacon of modern architecture and maritime guidance on the coast of Jeddah, Saudi Arabia. This towering lighthouse is not only the tallest in the world, reaching a remarkable height of 133 meters, but also an emblem of Jeddah's transformation into a major maritime hub. Situated on the northern edge of Jeddah's main harbor, this unique lighthouse is a striking white structure with a circular base, designed to serve both as a guiding light for ships and as a symbol of the city's growth and modernization. Its position at the Red Sea's gateway has made it an invaluable tool for navigation, ensuring safe passage for vessels entering Jeddah's bustling port.

Constructed in 1990, Jeddah Light was part of a broader initiative to upgrade Jeddah's port facilities, reflecting Saudi Arabia's ambition to become a global player in maritime trade. Its towering structure can be seen from miles away, and its powerful beam, which has a range of over 25 nautical miles, helps guide large cargo ships and tankers safely into the harbor. Built using reinforced concrete and featuring a futuristic design, Jeddah Light stands out not only for its height but also for its distinct circular observation deck, which adds a unique architectural touch to its otherwise minimalist appearance.

Jeddah is located on Saudi Arabia's western coast, along the eastern shore of the Red Sea. The city experiences a hot desert climate, with temperatures reaching above 40 degrees Celsius in the summer months, making it one of the warmest coastal areas in the region. Winters are milder, with temperatures around 20 to 25 degrees Celsius, providing some relief from the intense heat. Despite the challenging climate, the lighthouse's design and materials were chosen to withstand the extreme conditions of the Arabian Peninsula, including high humidity, salt, and sandstorms that frequently sweep across the coast.

As one of Jeddah's most distinctive landmarks, Jeddah Light attracts attention not only from seafarers but also from architecture enthusiasts and tourists. Though not open to the public, the lighthouse is admired from the harbor and nearby coastal areas. It has become a popular subject for photographers, especially during sunset, when the warm colors of the sky reflect off the Red Sea, creating a dramatic backdrop that highlights the lighthouse's towering silhouette. Its role extends beyond navigation, symbolizing the spirit of modernity and ambition that characterizes Jeddah and Saudi Arabia as a whole.

The coastal environment around Jeddah Light is relatively sparse in terms of vegetation, given the arid climate. However, the waters of the Red Sea are home to an extraordinary array of marine life, including coral reefs that rank among the most beautiful and diverse in the world. Dolphins are occasionally spotted near the coast, and the coral reefs attract divers from around the globe, eager to explore the rich underwater ecosystem. While the immediate area around the lighthouse is industrial due to the harbor's presence, the nearby sea remains a haven for marine biodiversity.

For the people of Jeddah, the lighthouse is more than a navigational aid; it represents the city's role as a gateway to Saudi Arabia and a focal point for international trade and commerce. The port is one of

LIGHTHOUSE: BEACON OF HISTORY AND LIGHT

the busiest in the region, serving as a critical entry point for goods bound for the entire Arabian Peninsula. Jeddah Light, in this sense, stands as a symbol of the city's economic importance and its openness to the world. For residents, it is a point of pride, embodying Jeddah's historical role as a port city and its future as a cosmopolitan center.

Despite its modern construction, Jeddah Light faces challenges associated with its harsh environment. The salt-laden air from the Red Sea accelerates corrosion, posing a continual maintenance challenge for the structure. Sandstorms, which are common in the region, can obscure visibility and affect the lighthouse's function temporarily. Additionally, the high temperatures and intense sunlight place significant stress on the materials, requiring regular inspections and repairs to ensure the lighthouse remains operational and visually striking.

One interesting fact about Jeddah Light is its architectural design, which combines functional efficiency with an aesthetic appeal that mirrors Saudi Arabia's modernization efforts. Unlike traditional lighthouses, Jeddah Light's design incorporates a circular observation deck that gives it a unique silhouette. It also stands as a testament to engineering ingenuity, as building such a tall structure on the coast required careful consideration of environmental stresses and the challenges of constructing in an arid climate. Its height and design have earned it the title of the world's tallest lighthouse, a point of distinction that adds to Jeddah's growing list of architectural achievements.

The importance of Jeddah Light extends far beyond its immediate surroundings. Positioned as one of the busiest shipping lanes in the world, it plays a crucial role in facilitating global trade. The Red Sea is a vital maritime route that connects Europe, Asia, and Africa, and Jeddah's port serves as a primary link in this chain. Ships from all over the world pass by Jeddah Light as they make their way to or from the Suez Canal, underscoring the lighthouse's role in supporting not only Saudi Arabia's economy but also international commerce. Its beam is a constant reminder of the critical role that lighthouses play in ensuring the safety and efficiency of global shipping networks.

The port of Jeddah is well-connected by various transportation options. Jeddah Islamic Port, near the lighthouse, serves as a major hub for goods entering and leaving the country. The nearby King Abdulaziz International Airport connects Jeddah to destinations worldwide, making it an accessible point for international trade. For tourists and visitors, the city offers a range of accommodations and transport options, making it easy to visit the coastline and admire the lighthouse from afar. The Red Sea coastline is also lined with promenades, shopping centers, and restaurants, allowing visitors to take in the views of Jeddah Light while enjoying the city's vibrant coastal life.

Standing tall over the Red Sea, Jeddah Light embodies the city's connection to the maritime world and its role as a gateway between continents. Its presence on the harbor is both practical and symbolic, representing Jeddah's long history as a port city and its place in the global economy. As one of the few modern lighthouses that rival ancient structures in stature, it captures the imagination of those who see it, offering a glimpse into the world of maritime navigation and the vision of a nation reaching for new heights. Jeddah Light will continue to stand as a beacon of progress, guiding ships safely and reminding visitors of the enduring importance of this iconic structure on the Saudi Arabian coast.

33. Kovalam Lighthouse - India

Perched atop a lush hill overlooking the azure waters of the Arabian Sea, Kovalam Lighthouse stands as a beacon of maritime heritage on the southwestern coast of India. Located in the small town of Kovalam, Kerala, this iconic lighthouse rises to a height of 35 meters, painted in bold red and white stripes that make it instantly recognizable against the surrounding landscape of swaying coconut palms and verdant greenery. Built in 1972, the lighthouse has since become an integral part of Kovalam's charm, attracting visitors from around the world who are captivated by its beauty, history, and the breathtaking views it offers of the coastline.

Kovalam Lighthouse is strategically situated on Lighthouse Beach, the largest of Kovalam's three crescent-shaped beaches, guiding ships navigating the Arabian Sea. Its elevated position on the rocky headland known as Kurumkal Hill gives it an impressive vantage point, allowing its beam of light to reach far out into the sea, warning vessels of the nearby shore and ensuring their safe passage. This placement is no coincidence; the area has a long history of maritime trade, and the lighthouse was built to support the thriving port activities along the

Malabar Coast, one of India's most important trading regions for centuries.

The climate in Kovalam is tropical, with warm and humid conditions prevailing throughout the year. Temperatures average between 25 and 30 degrees Celsius, with a relatively cooler period from November to February, which also marks the peak tourist season. Monsoon rains arrive from June to September, transforming the landscape into a lush green paradise but also bringing heavy downpours and choppy seas. The lighthouse, standing resiliently against the monsoon winds and rains, remains a symbol of stability in a region known for its intense weather patterns.

Kovalam Lighthouse is not only an essential navigational aid but also a popular tourist attraction. Its scenic location on the beach, combined with the opportunity to climb to the top and take in panoramic views of the Arabian Sea, makes it a must-visit destination for travelers exploring Kerala. From the observation deck, visitors can gaze out over the shoreline, spotting fishing boats bobbing in the waves and enjoying the cool sea breeze. The sight of the sun setting over the Arabian Sea from the top of the lighthouse is an experience cherished by many, adding to the allure of this coastal landmark.

The area surrounding the lighthouse is characterized by typical coastal flora, including coconut palms, casuarina trees, and various shrubs that thrive in the salty air and sandy soil. The nearby beaches are teeming with life, as seabirds like egrets, sandpipers, and seagulls can often be seen foraging along the shore or flying overhead. The Arabian Sea itself is home to a rich array of marine species, including vibrant coral reefs, tropical fish, and occasionally even dolphins, which delight visitors with their playful antics near the shore. The lush environment and biodiversity around the lighthouse contribute to the natural beauty of Kovalam, drawing nature enthusiasts and beach lovers alike.

For the people of Kovalam and the surrounding region, the lighthouse is more than just a navigational aid; it is a symbol of their community

LIGHTHOUSE: BEACON OF HISTORY AND LIGHT

and a link to the area's seafaring traditions. The Malabar Coast has a long history of maritime trade, with ancient links to cultures in the Middle East, Europe, and beyond. Local fishermen, who rely on the sea for their livelihood, have a deep respect for the lighthouse, as it guides them safely back to shore after long days spent at sea. It has become an enduring symbol of hope and homecoming, marking the coastline with its reassuring presence.

Maintaining Kovalam Lighthouse in the humid, coastal climate of Kerala presents its challenges. The high humidity, salty air, and frequent monsoon rains lead to faster corrosion of the metal components, and the structure requires regular maintenance to ensure it remains in good condition. Efforts to preserve the lighthouse include frequent painting, repairs to the masonry, and upgrading the lighting technology to ensure it continues to function effectively. Despite these challenges, the lighthouse stands strong, thanks to the dedication of those who work tirelessly to maintain it.

One lesser-known fact about Kovalam Lighthouse is that it was constructed with local materials and expertise, reflecting Kerala's rich tradition of craftsmanship. Unlike many older lighthouses that relied on imported materials, Kovalam Lighthouse's construction was a testament to the skills of local artisans and engineers. The structure's design is simple yet effective, built to withstand the coastal weather while blending seamlessly with the natural landscape. The red and white stripes, chosen for their high visibility, give the lighthouse a distinctive appearance that has become a beloved part of Kovalam's identity.

The importance of Kovalam Lighthouse extends beyond its role as a tourist attraction. Its beam, visible from nearly 30 kilometers out at sea, continues to serve as a crucial guide for vessels navigating the busy waters of the Arabian Sea. The Malabar Coast is an active maritime route, with ships transporting goods between India and destinations in the Middle East, Africa, and beyond. The lighthouse's steady beam is a welcome sight for sailors, providing reassurance as they approach the shore and warning them of the rocky coastline that has claimed many ships over the centuries.

Kovalam's accessibility by various modes of transport makes it a popular destination for both domestic and international travelers. Trivandrum International Airport, located about 16 kilometers away, connects Kovalam to major cities in India and abroad, while the nearby railway station in Thiruvananthapuram provides easy access by train. For those traveling by road, the well-maintained highways make the journey from nearby cities a scenic experience, passing through Kerala's lush landscapes and coastal views. The town's thriving tourism industry has also led to a range of accommodations, from luxurious beach resorts to budget-friendly guesthouses, catering to all types of travelers. Today, Kovalam Lighthouse stands as a symbol of Kerala's natural beauty, maritime heritage, and welcoming spirit. Its light continues to shine, guiding ships and inspiring visitors with its serene presence by the sea. For those who climb to the top, the view of the endless horizon and the sounds of the waves crashing below offer a sense of peace and connection to the timeless rhythm of the ocean. Kovalam Lighthouse is not merely a navigational structure; it is a cherished landmark that has become an inseparable part of the community, a beacon of guidance and inspiration that will continue to stand proudly on the shores of Kerala for generations to come.

34. La Corbière Lighthouse - Jersey (Channel Islands)

La Corbière Lighthouse, perched on a rugged islet off the southwestern coast of Jersey in the Channel Islands, stands as a dramatic sentinel against the vastness of the Atlantic Ocean. Built in 1874, this white cylindrical tower rises about 19 meters above its rocky base, guiding mariners safely past the treacherous reefs that surround the island. The lighthouse's location on a tidal island, accessible only during low tide via a narrow causeway, adds to its allure and mystique. Known for its exposed and isolated setting, La Corbière is one of the most photographed sites in Jersey, drawing visitors eager to witness its beauty and the powerful forces of nature that shape its surroundings.

Situated at the southwestern tip of Jersey, the largest of the Channel Islands, La Corbière is strategically positioned to guide ships around the island's rocky coastline. Jersey's location between the coasts of England and France has made it an important maritime landmark for centuries, and the waters around La Corbière are known for their strong tides, swift currents, and hidden reefs. The lighthouse was built to address the dangers posed by these natural hazards, providing a much-needed navigational aid to vessels navigating the English Channel.

The climate around La Corbière is typically maritime, with mild winters and cool summers. The island experiences frequent rainfall throughout the year, particularly during the autumn and winter months. Temperatures average around 15 to 20 degrees Celsius in the summer and rarely fall below 5 degrees Celsius in winter, making it a relatively temperate location. However, the lighthouse's exposed position on the coast means it often faces strong winds, especially during the winter months when storms roll in from the Atlantic, creating dramatic scenes as waves crash against the rocks and spray reaches the base of the tower.

La Corbière Lighthouse is not only essential for navigation but has also become a beloved landmark in Jersey. The causeway leading to the lighthouse is accessible at low tide, allowing visitors to walk across to the rocky islet where the lighthouse stands. This experience, combined with the breathtaking views of the ocean and coastline, has made La Corbière a popular destination for tourists and locals alike. Watching the sunset from La Corbière is a cherished activity, as the lighthouse and surrounding rocks are bathed in golden light, creating a scene of serene beauty and isolation. The area around the lighthouse is also a designated Ramsar Wetland site, highlighting its ecological importance and the need to preserve its unique coastal environment.

The flora and fauna around La Corbière are typical of the Channel Islands' coastal ecosystems. The rocky islet and nearby cliffs are home to hardy plants that thrive in the salty, windy environment, such as sea thrift, heather, and various grasses. The surrounding waters are rich in marine life, including fish, crustaceans, and seabirds that feed on the abundant resources of the Atlantic Ocean. Seagulls, fulmars, and cormorants are commonly seen around the lighthouse, and the rocks provide nesting sites for these seabirds. Occasionally, seals and even

LIGHTHOUSE: BEACON OF HISTORY AND LIGHT

dolphins can be spotted off the coast, adding to the natural allure of La Corbière.

For the people of Jersey, La Corbière Lighthouse holds a special place in their hearts. It has long been a symbol of the island's maritime heritage and resilience. The lighthouse's powerful beam, which can be seen from up to 18 miles away, has guided countless vessels safely past the island, and its presence provides a reassuring light in the darkness. La Corbière's name itself comes from the French word "corbeau," meaning "crow," likely referring to the dark rocks that surround the lighthouse. Over the years, the lighthouse has become an emblem of safety and strength, a place that connects Jersey's past with its present.

The challenges of maintaining La Corbière Lighthouse are considerable. Its remote location on a tidal island means that access is limited to periods of low tide, complicating maintenance and repairs. The harsh coastal environment, with salt-laden winds and frequent storms, accelerates wear on the structure, requiring regular upkeep to ensure it remains in good condition. Despite these difficulties, the lighthouse has withstood the test of time, thanks to the dedication of those who have worked to preserve it. Over the years, the lighthouse has been modernized, transitioning from oil lamps to electric light, and today it operates automatically, though its historical charm has been carefully preserved.

One intriguing aspect of La Corbière Lighthouse is its connection to a famous maritime rescue. In 1995, a ship named the "Saint-Malo" ran aground near La Corbière, and a rescue helicopter was dispatched to save the crew. The operation was a success, and the incident highlighted the continuing importance of the lighthouse in ensuring maritime safety. This event remains in local memory as a testament to the lighthouse's role as a guardian of the coast, watching over the waters and helping to prevent further tragedies.

The importance of La Corbière Lighthouse extends far beyond its immediate surroundings. The Channel Islands are located along one of the busiest shipping routes in the world, and La Corbière plays a crucial role in guiding vessels safely through the narrow strait between Jersey and the French coast. Its light has prevented countless shipwrecks, providing a safe passage for sailors navigating the challenging waters of the English Channel. Its significance as a navigational aid, combined with its historical and cultural value, makes La Corbière an irreplaceable part of Jersey's maritime heritage.

Jersey's accessibility by various transport modes makes La Corbière a popular destination for visitors from the UK, France, and beyond. Ferries from the nearby ports of St. Malo, France, and Portsmouth, England, connect Jersey to the mainland, while Jersey Airport offers flights to several major cities. Once on the island, visitors can easily reach La Corbière by car or bus, and the scenic coastal roads make the journey to the lighthouse an experience in itself. The area surrounding La Corbière is also popular for hiking, with trails offering stunning views of the coastline and the lighthouse in the distance.

Standing against the powerful forces of the Atlantic, La Corbière Lighthouse is a beacon of resilience and history. Its light, which has guided sailors for over a century, continues to shine, marking the edge of the Channel Islands with a symbol of hope and safety. For those who visit, La Corbière offers more than just a glimpse into maritime history; it provides a connection to the timeless beauty of the sea, the strength of the island community, and the enduring presence of a lighthouse that has become a beloved icon of Jersey. Whether viewed from the shore or up close during low tide, La Corbière Lighthouse remains a symbol of the island's heritage, a link to its maritime past, and a shining example of the enduring importance of lighthouses in guiding humanity through the challenges of the open sea.

35. Lindesnes Lighthouse - Norway

Lindesnes Lighthouse stands proudly on the southernmost point of Norway, marking the end of the Norwegian mainland and the gateway to the North Sea. Located at Lindesnes, this iconic lighthouse reaches a height of 16 meters, painted in classic white with a red lantern room at the top. Established in 1656, Lindesnes Lighthouse holds the distinction of being Norway's oldest lighthouse, built to guide ships through the dangerous waters between the North Sea and the Skagerrak Strait. Its location is as strategic as it is dramatic, perched on rugged cliffs where strong winds and turbulent seas meet the rocky coast, creating a scene that is as awe-inspiring as it is formidable.

The lighthouse was initially constructed as an essential navigational aid to address the increasing maritime traffic passing through the strait, connecting Norway with the rest of Europe. Over the centuries, Lindesnes Lighthouse has undergone numerous upgrades, shifting from a coal fire to an oil lamp, and finally to modern electric lighting. Its beacon, visible from 19 nautical miles away, has been a lifesaver for countless vessels navigating these challenging waters. The lighthouse's remote setting, far from urban development, makes it an isolated yet vital outpost, standing resiliently against the fierce elements that define Norway's coastal environment.

Located at the meeting point of the North Sea and the Skagerrak Strait, Lindesnes Lighthouse experiences a maritime climate, with cool summers and cold, often stormy winters. Temperatures in the summer months range between 10 and 20 degrees Celsius, while winter temperatures can drop below freezing, with powerful winds and occasional snow. The lighthouse's position exposes it to the full force of the North Sea gales, making winter particularly challenging for both the structure and the keepers who historically tended to it. Today, Lindesnes Lighthouse remains fully operational and automated to withstand the harsh conditions while continuing to serve as a vital navigational aid.

Lindesnes Lighthouse is not only a functional navigational tool but also a popular tourist destination, drawing thousands of visitors every year. The scenic location and historical significance of the lighthouse make it a favorite among travelers interested in Norway's maritime heritage. Visitors can explore the lighthouse and its surroundings, including a small museum that provides insights into the lighthouse's history and the life of the keepers who once called this remote station home. Climbing to the top of the lighthouse offers breathtaking panoramic views of the sea and coastline, and the powerful winds add to the sense of standing on the edge of the world. Sunsets viewed from Lindesnes are particularly spectacular, with the lighthouse silhouetted against the glowing horizon.

The natural landscape around Lindesnes is wild and unspoiled, with rocky cliffs, sparse vegetation, and mosses that cling to the rugged terrain. The coastline is characterized by granite rock formations, carved by centuries of wind and waves, creating a unique coastal wilderness. The flora in this region is limited due to the harsh conditions, but hardy grasses, heather, and low-lying shrubs manage to survive. The surrounding waters are rich in marine life, and seabirds,

LIGHTHOUSE: BEACON OF HISTORY AND LIGHT

including gulls and cormorants, are a common sight around the lighthouse, often seen diving into the sea or perching on the rocks. Occasionally, seals can be spotted along the shore, adding to the natural beauty of the area.

For the people of Norway, Lindesnes Lighthouse is a cherished symbol of their country's seafaring traditions and a testament to human resilience in the face of nature's challenges. It represents Norway's long-standing connection to the sea and the importance of maritime navigation for a country with such an extensive coastline. The lighthouse has been a part of Norway's history for over three centuries, witnessing the evolution of maritime technology and the changing needs of navigation. The lighthouse's status as a national landmark makes it a source of pride, and it has become a cultural icon, embodying the spirit of Norway's rugged coastline and adventurous heritage.

Maintaining Lindesnes Lighthouse in such an exposed location is no small feat. The salt-laden air and frequent storms cause wear and tear on the structure, requiring regular maintenance to preserve its functionality and historical value. In addition to the weather, the lighthouse's remote location poses logistical challenges, as supplies and materials must be transported across rough terrain to reach the site. However, the dedication to preserving this landmark remains strong, and restoration efforts are regularly undertaken to ensure that Lindesnes continues to stand as a beacon of Norwegian heritage and maritime safety.

An interesting historical fact about Lindesnes Lighthouse is that it was not always well-received by all sailors. In its early years, there was confusion among seafarers due to its similarity in appearance and light signal to the lighthouse at Skagen, Denmark. This led to several accidents, prompting the lighthouse keepers to change the light's characteristics. Today, Lindesnes is recognized for its distinctive flashing light, which has become an unmistakable symbol for mariners navigating this part of the world. Another intriguing detail is the network of underground tunnels built during World War II, when German forces occupied the area and fortified the lighthouse, adding a layer of wartime history to the site.

The importance of Lindesnes Lighthouse is profound, given its role in safeguarding one of Europe's most challenging maritime routes. The waters around Lindesnes are notorious for their strong currents and unpredictable weather, making navigation difficult even for experienced sailors. The lighthouse's beam provides a critical reference point for ships entering the Skagerrak Strait, helping to prevent accidents and guiding vessels safely along the coast. As the southernmost point of Norway, Lindesnes has been an essential stop for both commercial ships and fishing vessels, contributing to the safety and efficiency of maritime trade in the region.

Norway's extensive network of transportation makes Lindesnes Lighthouse accessible, despite its remote location. The nearest town, Mandal, is about 25 kilometers away and can be reached by road. From Mandal, visitors can travel by car or local transport to reach the lighthouse, following scenic coastal routes that showcase Norway's breathtaking landscape. While there are no major international routes directly passing the lighthouse, its proximity to key maritime routes in the North Sea underscores its significance for international shipping and fishing activities.

Standing at the southern tip of Norway, Lindesnes Lighthouse embodies the intersection of natural beauty, historical significance, and practical utility. For those who visit, the lighthouse offers a unique glimpse into Norway's maritime legacy and the rugged charm of its coastline. With each passing day, the lighthouse continues to fulfill its role, guiding ships through the challenges of the North Sea while serving as an enduring symbol of Norway's resilience and commitment to its maritime traditions. Lindesnes Lighthouse is not just a navigational aid; it is a piece of history, a beacon of hope, and a beloved

LIGHTHOUSE: BEACON OF HISTORY AND LIGHT

icon of Norway's southernmost point, capturing the essence of the sea and the spirit of exploration that defines this remarkable country.

36. Makapuʻu Point Lighthouse - USA

Makapuʻu Point Lighthouse stands majestically on the southeastern tip of Oahu, Hawaii, overlooking the vast expanse of the Pacific Ocean. Built in 1909, this small yet prominent lighthouse reaches a height of 14 meters and is perched on a 213-meter-high cliff, making it visible from a great distance out at sea. With its distinctive white tower and bright red top, the Makapuʻu Point Lighthouse has become an iconic sight, a symbol of maritime history nestled within Hawaii's natural beauty. Its strategic location provides a critical guide for ships navigating the treacherous waters around Oahu, safeguarding vessels approaching from both the open ocean and the Hawaiian archipelago. Located near the Makapuʻu Point Trail, the lighthouse occupies a prime vantage point that offers panoramic views of the ocean and coastline. From the cliffs, one can see not only the rugged Hawaiian coast but, on clear days, even the islands of Molokai and Lanai on the horizon. The lighthouse was originally built to improve maritime safety, as Oahu's rocky eastern shores presented a challenge to early sailors. Its establishment marked a significant advancement in

LIGHTHOUSE: BEACON OF HISTORY AND LIGHT

navigation for the region, helping ships avoid the dangerous reefs and currents that characterize the area.

The climate around Makapuʻu Point is tropical, with warm temperatures year-round. Average temperatures range between 24 and 30 degrees Celsius, creating a comfortable environment for visitors and locals alike. The area experiences a dry season from May to October, with gentle trade winds keeping the temperatures pleasant, while the rainy season from November to April brings sporadic showers. However, even during the rainy season, the weather remains mild and enjoyable, with the rains typically brief and followed by clear skies. The steady warmth and sunshine contribute to the lush vegetation and rich biodiversity surrounding the lighthouse, adding to the appeal of this scenic location.

Over the years, Makapuʻu Point Lighthouse has become a popular destination for tourists and hikers. The Makapuʻu Point Trail is a well-maintained path that leads visitors up to a viewpoint overlooking the lighthouse, offering breathtaking views of the coastline and ocean below. The trail is especially popular during winter months when it becomes one of the best spots on Oahu for whale watching. Humpback whales migrate to Hawaiian waters from December to April, and visitors to the lighthouse area are often treated to the sight of these magnificent creatures breaching and spouting in the distance. The combination of historical interest, natural beauty, and whale-watching opportunities has made Makapuʻu Point a beloved spot for locals and tourists alike.

The flora and fauna around Makapuʻu Point reflect Hawaii's unique ecosystem. The cliffs are covered with native plants like the Hawaiian ʻIlima and Naupaka, which thrive in the rocky, sun-drenched environment. Coastal seabirds, such as the wedge-tailed shearwater and red-footed booby, can often be seen gliding over the ocean or resting on the cliffs, taking advantage of the strong updrafts along the shore. The ocean below is home to a variety of marine life, including dolphins and, during the winter season, humpback whales that migrate to the warm Hawaiian waters to breed. The surrounding natural beauty enhances the lighthouse's charm, making it a part of the vibrant Hawaiian landscape.

Makapu'u Point Lighthouse holds a special place in the hearts of the Hawaiian people, symbolizing both their connection to the sea and the island's role as a navigational landmark in the Pacific. Built during a time when Hawaii was still a U.S. territory, the lighthouse reflects the island's integration into the maritime routes of the Pacific. For locals, the lighthouse is more than just a navigational aid; it represents a link to Hawaii's past, a reminder of the time when these shores were not only home to native Hawaiians but also an important stopover for voyaging ships and whalers. The lighthouse has thus become a part of Hawaii's cultural fabric, celebrated as a landmark that connects the past with the present.

Maintaining the lighthouse has posed unique challenges, given its isolated and elevated position. The steep cliffs and rugged terrain make accessing the lighthouse a challenge, especially for maintenance crews who must bring equipment and materials up the narrow paths. The salt air and constant exposure to the elements accelerate corrosion, necessitating frequent repairs to keep the structure in good condition. Despite these challenges, the lighthouse remains operational, thanks to the dedication of those who work to preserve its historical and functional value. In recent years, efforts have focused on conserving not only the lighthouse itself but also the surrounding area, ensuring that future generations can continue to enjoy this remarkable site.

One interesting fact about Makapu'u Point Lighthouse is that it houses one of the largest Fresnel lenses in the United States. This massive lens, made in France and installed in 1909, is a hyper-radial Fresnel lens with a diameter of nearly two meters. Its size and power are what give the lighthouse its impressive range, allowing the light to be seen up to 28 miles away. Although the lighthouse has since

LIGHTHOUSE: BEACON OF HISTORY AND LIGHT

been automated and the original light source replaced with modern technology, the historic Fresnel lens remains a defining feature of Makapuʻu, symbolizing the ingenuity and craftsmanship that went into its construction.

The significance of Makapuʻu Point Lighthouse extends beyond its role as a navigational aid. As one of the most easterly points on Oahu, it serves as a crucial guide for ships traveling to and from the Hawaiian Islands. The Pacific Ocean is vast, and the Hawaiian Islands are relatively isolated, making landmarks like Makapuʻu essential for safe passage. The lighthouse has helped countless vessels navigate these waters, preventing shipwrecks and supporting trade and travel across the Pacific. Its beam stands as a testament to the enduring need for guidance and safety on the open sea.

Oahu's accessibility by air and sea makes Makapuʻu Point Lighthouse a feasible destination for visitors from around the world. Honolulu International Airport connects Oahu to major cities in the United States and Asia, while a network of highways and public transportation allows easy access to the lighthouse from Honolulu and other parts of the island. For those looking to explore the area on foot, the Makapuʻu Point Trail is accessible by car and provides a pleasant and scenic hike up to the viewpoint. The lighthouse's location on Oahu's southeastern coast places it within reach of other popular attractions, making it a perfect stop for tourists exploring the island's natural beauty and historical sites.

Today, Makapuʻu Point Lighthouse remains a beloved symbol of Hawaii's maritime heritage and natural beauty. Its light continues to shine over the Pacific, guiding ships and inspiring visitors with its presence on the rugged Hawaiian cliffs. For those who make the journey to Makapuʻu, the lighthouse offers more than just a view; it provides a connection to Hawaii's past, a link to the wider world, and a reminder of the enduring power of light and guidance in the vastness of the ocean. Standing tall on the cliff's edge, Makapuʻu Point

MD SHAR

Lighthouse captures the spirit of Hawaii—a place of beauty, resilience, and endless horizons.

37. Malaga Lighthouse - Spain

La Farola de Málaga, affectionately known as "La Farola," stands proudly on the bustling coastline of Málaga, Spain. Erected in 1817, this 38-meter-tall cylindrical white tower is a cherished symbol of the city and one of the few lighthouses in Spain with a feminine name. Located on the harbor, where the Guadalmedina River meets the Mediterranean Sea, La Farola has guided countless ships safely into Málaga's port, playing a crucial role in the maritime history of the region.

The lighthouse was designed by Joaquín María Pery y Guzmán, an engineer who envisioned it as an essential navigational aid for the harbor. During the early 19th century, Málaga was an important port in the Mediterranean, drawing ships from across Europe and beyond. The lighthouse was built to address the growing maritime traffic, ensuring vessels could safely navigate the coast's rocky waters. Over two centuries, La Farola has witnessed the transformation of Málaga from a historic trading port to a modern city while remaining a steadfast landmark, bridging past and present.

Málaga's coastal climate is Mediterranean, with hot, dry summers and mild winters. From June to September, temperatures average between 25 and 35 degrees Celsius, with clear skies and warm sea breezes that draw locals and tourists to the beaches. Winters, from December to February, are cooler, with temperatures around 15 to 20 degrees Celsius, often accompanied by sporadic rain showers. La Farola, standing resiliently against the seasonal changes, is particularly captivating at sunset when the golden hues cast by the sun on its white tower create an ethereal glow against the blue waters of the Mediterranean.

Over the years, La Farola has become more than a beacon for ships; it is a beloved icon of Málaga and a popular spot for visitors. Positioned along the scenic harbor promenade, it attracts tourists who come to photograph its elegant structure, take in the surrounding views, and explore the vibrant coastal area. With nearby cafes, shops, and the Mediterranean's soft waves lapping against the shore, La Farola's presence contributes to Málaga's charming and inviting atmosphere. Locals often take leisurely strolls along the harbor, with the lighthouse serving as a tranquil backdrop, enhancing the beauty and serenity of the Andalusian coast.

The area around La Farola is teeming with Mediterranean flora, including palm trees, oleander, and bougainvillea, which add vibrant colors to the landscape. These plants thrive in the warm climate, framing the lighthouse and creating an idyllic coastal scene. Seagulls are a frequent sight around La Farola, often seen soaring above or resting along the harbor walls. Occasionally, dolphins can be spotted in the waters nearby, delighting onlookers with their playful behavior. The lighthouse's location, surrounded by both urban life and natural beauty, exemplifies the harmonious blend of Málaga's coastal ecosystem and the bustling port.

For the people of Málaga, La Farola is a cultural treasure and a source of pride. Its image is seen in local art, souvenirs, and city branding,

LIGHTHOUSE: BEACON OF HISTORY AND LIGHT

symbolizing Málaga's maritime heritage and its connection to the Mediterranean. The lighthouse has become an integral part of the community, representing the resilience and openness of the city. Over generations, La Farola has stood as a silent witness to Málaga's growth, bearing witness to historical events, economic changes, and the ebb and flow of life along the coast.

Despite its enduring charm, maintaining La Farola has been challenging. The salt air and proximity to the sea accelerate wear on its structure, requiring regular maintenance to protect it from corrosion. Additionally, during the Spanish Civil War in the 1930s, La Farola was damaged by bombings, leading to extensive repairs and upgrades that included modern lighting technology. The lighthouse has since been restored multiple times, with efforts focused on preserving its historical integrity while adapting it to contemporary needs. Today, La Farola remains fully operational, and automated to continue serving the port while retaining its classic design.

One interesting fact about La Farola is that it was only the second lighthouse built on the Mediterranean coast of Spain. This distinction adds to its historical significance, marking it as an important part of Spain's early lighthouse network. Its unique feminine name, "La Farola," sets it apart from most other lighthouses, which are typically referred to with masculine terms. This naming convention has endeared it to locals, who regard La Farola with a sense of affection and reverence, considering it almost as a part of the family.

La Farola's significance extends beyond Málaga's harbor; it is a crucial navigational aid for ships traveling along the busy Mediterranean routes. The Port of Málaga, one of the oldest continuously operating ports in Europe, has long served as a gateway between Europe, North Africa, and the Middle East. The lighthouse plays a vital role in ensuring the safe arrival of vessels, particularly during challenging weather conditions or at night. Its light, visible for up to 25 nautical miles, provides a reassuring guide for captains as they approach the port, contributing to the region's economic activity and fostering international trade.

Málaga is well-connected by various transportation options, making La Farola accessible to visitors from around the world. Málaga-Costa del Sol Airport offers flights to numerous international destinations, and the city's high-speed train links it to Madrid and other major Spanish cities. The port itself welcomes cruise ships and ferries, further increasing Málaga's accessibility. For those exploring the area, public transport and walking paths make it easy to reach the lighthouse and the surrounding attractions. Positioned within reach of the city's historic center, beaches, and cultural sites, La Farola is a natural addition to any visit to Málaga.

Today, La Farola remains a beloved symbol of Málaga, embodying the city's spirit and resilience. Its light continues to shine over the Mediterranean, guiding ships and inspiring those who visit its shores. For locals, La Farola is more than just a lighthouse; it is a reminder of their connection to the sea and a witness to the evolution of their city. For visitors, it offers a glimpse into Málaga's maritime past and a chance to experience the timeless beauty of the Andalusian coast. La Farola de Málaga stands as a testament to the enduring importance of lighthouses, a beacon of safety, and a cultural landmark that will continue to illuminate Málaga's coast for generations to come.

38. Montauk Point Lighthouse - USA

Montauk Point Lighthouse stands proudly on the eastern tip of Long Island, New York, a timeless sentinel overlooking the Atlantic Ocean. Established in 1796, it is New York's oldest lighthouse and one of the first in the United States, a symbol of maritime heritage and an enduring guide for sailors navigating the often treacherous waters near Montauk. The lighthouse rises to a height of 34 meters and features a striking white and red tower that has become an iconic image on Long Island's coastline. Perched atop a cliff, Montauk Point Lighthouse offers an impressive view of the ocean, its beam reaching as far as 19 nautical miles, providing reassurance to those at sea.

The need for Montauk Point Lighthouse arose from the growing maritime activity along the East Coast in the late 18th century. The waters near Montauk were particularly perilous, with strong currents and shifting sands posing dangers to ships. President George Washington commissioned the construction of the lighthouse, recognizing its importance in safeguarding lives and supporting commerce. Completed in 1796, the lighthouse has stood through the changes of time, surviving storms, wars, and technological advancements. Today, it is a National Historic Landmark, celebrated for its historical and architectural significance.

Located on Long Island's easternmost point, Montauk Point Lighthouse is situated in a region known for its temperate climate. Summers are warm, with temperatures averaging around 25 degrees Celsius, and the cool sea breeze provides relief from the heat. Winters are colder, with temperatures often dropping to around 0 degrees Celsius, and occasional snowstorms sweeping across the coastline. The lighthouse faces the full force of Atlantic storms, particularly during the winter months, when strong winds and waves crash against the cliffs. Yet, through these challenges, Montauk Point Lighthouse stands resilient, a testament to its sturdy construction and historical significance.

Montauk Point Lighthouse is one of Long Island's most popular attractions, drawing visitors year-round who are captivated by its history, architecture, and scenic location. The surrounding area offers beautiful views of the Atlantic, and the lighthouse's elevated position provides a vantage point for observing the coastline and sea. Inside, visitors can explore a small museum detailing the lighthouse's history, including artifacts, old photographs, and stories of the lighthouse keepers who once tended to its light. Climbing the narrow stairs to the top rewards visitors with panoramic views of the ocean, a sight that has inspired generations of travelers.

The landscape around the lighthouse is characterized by grassy fields and rocky shores, typical of Long Island's coastal ecosystem. Native vegetation, including beach grasses and wildflowers, thrives in the salty, windswept environment, adding natural beauty to the area. Seagulls are a constant presence around the lighthouse, often seen circling above or perched on the cliffs. In the waters below, seals can sometimes be spotted lounging on the rocks or swimming along the shore, and during the annual whale migration, lucky visitors may catch a glimpse of whales breaching in the distance.

LIGHTHOUSE: BEACON OF HISTORY AND LIGHT

For the people of Montauk and Long Island, Montauk Point Lighthouse is more than just a navigational aid; it is a symbol of their community and maritime heritage. Over the centuries, the lighthouse has been a constant in the lives of those who live by the sea, providing a sense of security and connection to the island's history. The lighthouse has also played a role in local legends and folklore, further embedding it in the cultural fabric of the area. Today, it stands as a cherished landmark, a reminder of Montauk's seafaring past and its place in the history of the United States.

Maintaining Montauk Point Lighthouse has not been without challenges. The salty air and exposure to the elements cause wear on the structure, necessitating regular upkeep to preserve its historical integrity. Coastal erosion has also posed a significant threat to the lighthouse, as the cliffs upon which it stands have gradually receded over time. To combat this, the community and preservationists have undertaken efforts to protect the site, including reinforcement of the cliffs and restoration projects aimed at ensuring the lighthouse's survival for future generations. Despite these obstacles, Montauk Point Lighthouse continues to shine brightly, thanks to the dedication of those committed to its preservation.

An interesting fact about Montauk Point Lighthouse is its role during World War II. The U.S. military used the lighthouse as a lookout point, installing radar and using it as part of the coastal defense system. This added a new chapter to its history, as the lighthouse became a vital part of the war effort, helping to monitor the surrounding waters and detect any potential threats. The radar equipment is long gone, but the stories of the lighthouse's role during the war have become part of its legacy, reflecting its adaptability and importance through different periods of American history.

Montauk Point Lighthouse's significance as a navigational aid remains crucial, even with modern technology. The waters near Montauk are part of a busy shipping route, with vessels traveling along the East

Coast or crossing the Atlantic. The lighthouse's beam is a reassuring presence for sailors, a reminder of the importance of traditional navigation in an era dominated by GPS and digital systems. Its historical legacy, combined with its practical role, makes Montauk Point Lighthouse a rare blend of the past and present, embodying both nostalgia and functionality.

Montauk is accessible by various transportation options, including highways, trains, and ferries, making the lighthouse an easy destination for locals and tourists alike. The Long Island Rail Road connects Montauk to New York City, offering a scenic journey across the island. For those driving, the Montauk Highway provides direct access to the area. The nearby harbor also accommodates ferries, connecting Montauk with neighboring areas and adding to the town's appeal as a travel destination. The convenience of these transport options has made Montauk Point Lighthouse a popular stop for visitors exploring the natural and cultural attractions of Long Island.

Today, Montauk Point Lighthouse stands as a proud symbol of resilience and history. Its light continues to guide ships, and its presence draws countless visitors to the eastern tip of Long Island, where the ocean meets the land in a dramatic display of nature's power and beauty. For those who visit, Montauk Point Lighthouse offers a glimpse into America's maritime past, a connection to the lives of the lighthouse keepers who once called it home, and an appreciation for the enduring importance of lighthouses. This historic beacon, with its steadfast light, will continue to illuminate the coast, inspiring and guiding those who come to marvel at its strength and grace.

39. Peggy's Point Lighthouse - Canada

Peggy's Point Lighthouse, standing gracefully on the rugged shores of Peggy's Cove in Nova Scotia, Canada, is one of the most iconic lighthouses in North America. Built in 1915, this modest yet striking lighthouse rises to a height of 15 meters and is instantly recognizable by its classic white tower topped with a bright red lantern room. Set against a dramatic landscape of wave-smoothed granite boulders and the vast Atlantic Ocean, Peggy's Point Lighthouse has become a beloved symbol of Canada's maritime heritage, attracting visitors from around the world who come to experience the natural beauty and historical significance of this coastal landmark.

Located in the small fishing village of Peggy's Cove, the lighthouse marks the eastern entrance of St. Margaret's Bay, a body of water notorious for its jagged coastline and unpredictable weather. For over a century, Peggy's Point Lighthouse has guided sailors safely past the rocky shores, its light casting a reassuring glow across the bay. Its strategic location was carefully chosen to address the navigational challenges of the area, where strong tides and hidden rocks posed constant dangers to early sailors. Today, the lighthouse continues to serve as a crucial beacon, though it has also become a prominent tourist destination, drawing photographers, artists, and travelers alike.

The climate around Peggy's Cove is typically maritime, with cool, damp conditions prevailing throughout much of the year. Summers are mild, with temperatures averaging around 20 degrees Celsius, while winters are cold and often stormy, with temperatures hovering around freezing. The region experiences frequent fog, especially in the spring and fall, creating an ethereal atmosphere around the lighthouse. This fog, combined with the strong Atlantic winds and waves, has made Peggy's Cove a challenging but picturesque location, with the lighthouse standing as a resilient figure against the forces of nature.

Peggy's Point Lighthouse is one of Canada's most visited attractions, with tourists flocking to Peggy's Cove year-round to take in the stunning coastal scenery and the charm of the small fishing village. The lighthouse's unique position on a bed of granite boulders allows visitors to walk right up to its base, making it a popular spot for photographs and sightseeing. Despite its modest size, the lighthouse holds an outsized presence, its classic design embodying the rugged beauty of Nova Scotia's coastline. Visitors to Peggy's Cove can explore the rocks surrounding the lighthouse, listen to the waves crashing below, and take in the vastness of the Atlantic stretching out to the horizon.

The rocky landscape around Peggy's Point is a unique ecosystem, with hardy plants like wild roses, bayberry, and beach grass thriving in the cracks between the boulders. These resilient species are adapted to the harsh coastal conditions, clinging to the granite and adding a touch of green to the otherwise stark landscape. Seabirds such as gulls, cormorants, and terns frequent the area, often seen swooping over the waves or resting on the rocks. Occasionally, seals can be spotted in the waters near Peggy's Cove, and during certain times of the year, whale sightings are reported offshore, adding to the area's natural appeal.

For the people of Nova Scotia, Peggy's Point Lighthouse is more than a navigational aid; it is a beloved part of their cultural identity.

LIGHTHOUSE: BEACON OF HISTORY AND LIGHT

Generations of locals have grown up with the lighthouse as a backdrop to their lives, and its image has become synonymous with the province's coastal charm. The lighthouse represents a connection to the sea, which has been a lifeline for the fishing communities that dot the coast. It is a place of nostalgia and pride, a reminder of the challenges and beauty of coastal life in the Maritimes. The lighthouse's popularity has also contributed to the local economy, as tourism has become an essential part of the region's identity.

Maintaining Peggy's Point Lighthouse has been a challenging task, given its exposure to the elements. The harsh salt air, frequent storms, and high humidity accelerate the wear and tear on the structure, requiring regular maintenance to preserve its appearance and functionality. Over the years, the lighthouse has undergone several renovations, including upgrades to its lighting and structure to ensure it remains in good condition. The powerful waves and changing tides also pose a risk to the surrounding rocks, making safety a priority for visitors exploring the rugged coastline.

One lesser-known fact about Peggy's Point Lighthouse is that the original light source was a kerosene oil lamp, which was manually tended by lighthouse keepers. The light was later converted to electricity, and today, the lighthouse operates automatically, though its historical character has been carefully preserved. Another interesting tidbit is the story behind the name "Peggy's Cove," which, according to local legend, was named after a young girl who survived a shipwreck nearby. Known as "Peggy," she became a beloved figure in the village, and her story has been woven into the folklore of the area.

The significance of Peggy's Point Lighthouse extends beyond its role as a navigational tool. As a landmark, it serves as a reminder of Canada's maritime history, embodying the resilience and resourcefulness of coastal communities. Its light has guided countless ships safely into St. Margaret's Bay, and its presence has become a symbol of hope and guidance for sailors navigating the Atlantic's often turbulent waters.

Its location on the Atlantic Coast, where ships from Europe and the Americas have passed for centuries, places Peggy's Point Lighthouse at a crossroads of international maritime routes, underscoring its role in global navigation.

Peggy's Cove is accessible by various modes of transportation, making it a convenient destination for both domestic and international visitors. The nearest major airport is Halifax Stanfield International Airport, which connects Nova Scotia to cities across Canada and the United States. From Halifax, the drive to Peggy's Cove is a scenic journey along the Lighthouse Route, a coastal highway that offers breathtaking views of the Atlantic. Local buses and tour companies also provide transportation options, making it easy for tourists to visit Peggy's Point Lighthouse and experience the charm of Nova Scotia's coast.

Today, Peggy's Point Lighthouse stands as a beacon of Canada's maritime heritage and a beloved symbol of the East Coast. Its light continues to shine over the Atlantic, guiding ships and inspiring those who visit its shores. For locals and tourists alike, the lighthouse offers a chance to connect with the past, to appreciate the beauty of nature, and to experience the tranquility that comes from standing at the edge of the ocean. As one of Canada's most photographed and cherished landmarks, Peggy's Point Lighthouse will continue to captivate and guide generations, embodying the spirit of Nova Scotia's rugged coastline and the timeless appeal of lighthouses around the world.

40. Phare des Baleines - France

Phare des Baleines, or "Lighthouse of the Whales," stands proudly on the western tip of Île de Ré in France, overlooking the vast expanse of the Atlantic Ocean. Towering at a height of 57 meters, this stone lighthouse was completed in 1854, making it one of France's oldest and most revered coastal landmarks. Its name, Phare des Baleines, translates to "Lighthouse of the Whales" due to the whales that were once seen in the nearby waters, adding a sense of mystery and maritime romance to its legacy. The lighthouse's strategic location on the island provides essential guidance to vessels navigating the tricky waters of the Bay of Biscay and the French Atlantic coast.

The lighthouse was constructed to replace an earlier tower built in 1682 by order of King Louis XIV. The original lighthouse, now known as the "Old Tower," still stands nearby and serves as a historical monument, a silent witness to centuries of maritime history. The Phare des Baleines was designed to offer greater height and visibility, ensuring that ships could avoid the treacherous sandbanks and strong currents in the surrounding waters. Its stone structure, elegantly tapering toward the lantern room, combines both functionality and architectural beauty, standing as a beacon of safety and a marvel of 19th-century engineering.

Île de Ré enjoys a temperate oceanic climate, with mild winters and warm summers. In winter, temperatures average between 5 and 10 degrees Celsius, while summers are pleasant with averages around 20 to 25 degrees Celsius. The Atlantic Ocean has a moderating effect, keeping temperatures relatively stable year-round. However, strong winds and heavy rainfall are common during winter storms, when the waves crash dramatically against the island's shores. Despite these challenging conditions, Phare des Baleines stands resilient, its light cutting through fog, rain, and mist to ensure the safe passage of ships.

Today, Phare des Baleines is one of the most visited lighthouses in France, drawing thousands of visitors annually who are captivated by its history, architecture, and scenic location. Tourists can climb its 257 steps to reach the top, where they are rewarded with panoramic views of the island, the Atlantic Ocean, and the picturesque French coastline. From this vantage point, visitors can appreciate the island's salt marshes, sandy beaches, and charming villages that define Île de Ré's landscape. The nearby Old Tower and the surrounding lighthouse museum add to the experience, offering insights into the lighthouse's history and its role in France's maritime heritage.

The area around Phare des Baleines is rich in coastal flora and fauna. The island's ecosystem includes sandy dunes, salt marshes, and low-lying vegetation adapted to the salty air and wind. Sea lavender, wild thyme, and coastal grasses grow in the area, creating a lush, green contrast against the gray stones of the lighthouse. The Atlantic Ocean is home to a diverse array of marine life, and seabirds such as gulls, terns, and cormorants are commonly seen around the lighthouse, taking advantage of the updrafts along the cliff edges. During certain times of the year, seals and dolphins can be spotted in the waters nearby, adding to the island's natural charm.

LIGHTHOUSE: BEACON OF HISTORY AND LIGHT

For the people of Île de Ré, Phare des Baleines is a source of pride and a treasured landmark. It represents not only a link to France's seafaring past but also a symbol of the island's resilience and connection to the sea. The lighthouse has inspired local art, literature, and even folklore, making it an integral part of the island's identity. It serves as a gathering place for both locals and tourists, a site where the beauty of the island's natural landscape and its rich history converge. In recent years, the lighthouse has also become a symbol of environmental awareness, as local efforts to protect the island's ecosystem have grown alongside the lighthouse's popularity.

Maintaining Phare des Baleines is no small feat, given its exposure to the Atlantic's harsh conditions. Salt air, wind, and the occasional storm all take their toll on the stone and metal structures, necessitating frequent maintenance to ensure their preservation. Additionally, the increased foot traffic from visitors has led to the implementation of conservation measures to protect both the lighthouse and the surrounding environment. Preservation efforts have focused on reinforcing the structure, updating the lighting technology, and maintaining the surrounding landscape, all while respecting the historical integrity of this cherished landmark.

One fascinating detail about Phare des Baleines is its Fresnel lens, a technological marvel of its time. Invented by French physicist Augustin-Jean Fresnel, this lens system allows light to be visible over great distances. The Phare des Baleines' lens was designed to maximize visibility, and its powerful light has been a lifesaver for countless vessels navigating the unpredictable waters of the Atlantic. The Fresnel lens remains one of the defining features of the lighthouse, a reminder of the ingenuity and craftsmanship that went into its construction.

The significance of Phare des Baleines extends beyond its function as a navigational aid. As part of a network of lighthouses along the French coast, it has played a crucial role in supporting France's maritime economy by ensuring safe passage for ships entering and leaving the

Bay of Biscay. The lighthouse has seen the passage of merchant ships, fishing vessels, and even military fleets, marking its importance in both peacetime and wartime. Its light has guided generations of sailors and continues to serve as a testament to France's rich maritime history.

Île de Ré is well-connected by various modes of transportation, making Phare des Baleines an accessible destination for visitors from around the world. The island is connected to mainland France by a bridge, allowing easy access by car from the nearby city of La Rochelle. The La Rochelle Airport offers flights to major cities in France and Europe, and the island is also reachable by ferry. For those exploring the area, bicycle paths and walking trails provide scenic routes around the island, with the lighthouse as a natural highlight.

Today, Phare des Baleines stands as a beacon of history, resilience, and beauty. Its light continues to shine over the Atlantic, guiding ships and inspiring those who visit its shores. For locals and tourists alike, the lighthouse offers a connection to the past, a place of quiet reflection, and a chance to experience the timeless beauty of Île de Ré. Phare des Baleines is more than just a lighthouse; it is a symbol of France's enduring relationship with the sea, a reminder of the importance of maritime safety, and a cherished landmark that will continue to inspire future generations.

41. Point Reyes Lighthouse - USA

Point Reyes Lighthouse stands on a rugged cliff along the California coast, a steadfast sentinel overlooking the turbulent waters of the Pacific Ocean. Situated in Point Reyes National Seashore, about 30 miles northwest of San Francisco, the lighthouse was constructed in 1870 to guide ships past one of the most hazardous coastal areas in the United States. Its compact structure—just 16 meters tall—may seem small, but its location, atop a steep cliff that plunges into the ocean, makes it one of the most dramatic and iconic lighthouses on the West Coast. With its white walls and distinctive red roof, the Point Reyes Lighthouse has become a beloved landmark and a place of reflection for visitors who marvel at its rugged beauty and historical significance. In the 19th century, maritime travel along the California coast was perilous due to strong winds, shifting currents, and dense fog that often shrouded the area. Point Reyes, with its rocky coastline and intense weather, posed particular dangers to vessels making their way to and from San Francisco Bay. Recognizing the need for navigational aid, the U.S. Lighthouse Service chose the prominent Point Reyes headland to build a lighthouse that would help protect ships from treacherous conditions. After its completion in 1870, Point Reyes Lighthouse provided a much-needed beacon, its powerful Fresnel lens projecting light across the foggy waters.

Point Reyes experiences a maritime climate, with cool, foggy summers and mild winters. Summer temperatures average between 12 and 18 degrees Celsius, often accompanied by thick coastal fog, which adds an air of mystery and isolation to the lighthouse. Winters are slightly warmer and wetter, with temperatures ranging from 8 to 15 degrees Celsius. The fog and strong winds that characterize the area are integral to the landscape, and the lighthouse's construction took these conditions into account, with reinforced walls and a compact design to withstand the powerful gusts that batter the headland.

Despite its isolated location, Point Reyes Lighthouse is a popular destination, drawing thousands of visitors each year who are captivated by its scenic views, history, and natural surroundings. A steep 300-step staircase leads from the visitor center to the lighthouse, providing an opportunity to experience the dramatic landscape up close. The trek down the stairs, though challenging, is rewarded with breathtaking views of the Pacific and the satisfaction of reaching this historic structure. Many visitors come to watch the sunset or, in winter, to observe the migrating gray whales that pass through the waters just off the coast. The lighthouse has become a place of inspiration and contemplation, a testament to the enduring allure of the sea and the coast.

The surrounding cliffs and hills of Point Reyes are covered with coastal vegetation, including hardy grasses, wildflowers, and shrubs that thrive in the salty air and wind. The area is home to a diverse array of wildlife, from seabirds like gulls and pelicans that soar over the cliffs to marine animals such as seals and sea lions that inhabit the waters below. During the winter months, gray whales migrate along the coast, a sight that draws wildlife enthusiasts from around the region. The harsh coastal environment, with its salty air, fog, and constant winds, has shaped

LIGHTHOUSE: BEACON OF HISTORY AND LIGHT

the ecosystem around the lighthouse, creating a unique habitat that supports an impressive range of flora and fauna.

For the people of California and the surrounding communities, Point Reyes Lighthouse is more than a navigational aid; it is a cherished landmark and a symbol of the state's maritime heritage. Generations of Californians have visited the lighthouse, drawn by its remote beauty and the sense of solitude it offers. The lighthouse has also played a role in the lives of local fishermen and mariners, serving as a reliable guide through fog and storms. Its presence is a source of pride for the community, embodying the rugged and resilient spirit of the California coast.

Maintaining Point Reyes Lighthouse has been challenging, given its exposure to harsh coastal conditions. The salt air accelerates corrosion, and the intense winds can damage the structure over time. Additionally, the fog and cold weather create a damp environment that requires frequent maintenance to prevent deterioration. Despite these challenges, the National Park Service has undertaken numerous restoration projects to preserve the lighthouse, ensuring that it remains an operational and historical landmark for future generations. The 300-step staircase leading to the lighthouse is also maintained regularly to provide safe access for visitors.

One interesting fact about Point Reyes Lighthouse is its Fresnel lens, a technological marvel of the 19th century. The lens, imported from France, was designed to focus light into a powerful beam that could penetrate the dense fog surrounding Point Reyes. This lens allowed the lighthouse to be seen from up to 24 miles away, a vital improvement for ships navigating the dangerous coastal waters. The Fresnel lens remains a defining feature of the lighthouse, symbolizing the innovation and craftsmanship that went into its construction.

The importance of Point Reyes Lighthouse extends beyond its function as a navigational tool. Located along one of the busiest maritime routes in the Pacific, it has played a crucial role in ensuring the safety of vessels traveling to and from San Francisco Bay. The lighthouse's beam has guided countless ships through fog and storms, preventing accidents and saving lives. Its historical significance and its continued operation make Point Reyes Lighthouse a vital part of California's maritime infrastructure and a testament to the value of traditional navigation aids.

Point Reyes is accessible by road, and the lighthouse is a popular stop for visitors exploring Point Reyes National Seashore. The nearest town, Point Reyes Station, is about 12 miles away, providing accommodations and amenities for travelers. San Francisco, located about 30 miles to the south, is easily reachable by car, making Point Reyes Lighthouse a feasible day trip for tourists visiting the Bay Area. Public transportation options are limited, but many visitors choose to drive along the scenic coastal highways to reach the lighthouse and the surrounding park.

Today, Point Reyes Lighthouse stands as a beacon of history, resilience, and natural beauty. Its light continues to guide ships, while its presence draws countless visitors to California's rugged coast, where the land meets the powerful Pacific. For those who make the journey to Point Reyes, the lighthouse offers more than just a view; it provides a connection to California's maritime past, a place of solitude, and a chance to experience the raw beauty of the coast. Point Reyes Lighthouse remains a symbol of the unyielding power of the sea and the enduring legacy of those who built and maintained this vital beacon. Standing strong against the elements, it will continue to shine brightly, inspiring and guiding generations to come.

42. Portland Head Light - USA

Portland Head Light, located on the rocky cliffs of Cape Elizabeth, Maine, is one of the oldest and most iconic lighthouses in the United States. Established in 1791, this historic lighthouse stands at a height of 80 feet (24 meters), its white tower topped with a classic black lantern room. Its prime position on the edge of the Atlantic Ocean has made it a crucial navigational aid for mariners, guiding them safely into Portland Harbor for over two centuries. The lighthouse's picturesque setting, combined with its rich history, has made it a beloved symbol of Maine's maritime heritage and a popular destination for tourists and locals alike.

The construction of Portland Head Light was commissioned by President George Washington, recognizing the need for a beacon to warn ships of the rocky Maine coast. At the time, Portland was a bustling seaport, and the dangerous waters around Cape Elizabeth posed a significant threat to vessels. The lighthouse was built using local stones and materials, and when it was first lit on January 10, 1791, its whale oil lamps provided a crucial light that would later be replaced by a more powerful Fresnel lens. Over the years, the lighthouse has undergone numerous upgrades, including electrification, but it has retained its original character, standing as a testament to the craftsmanship of the early builders.

Cape Elizabeth, where Portland Head Light is situated, experiences a cool, temperate climate, with harsh winters and mild, breezy summers. Winter temperatures often hover around freezing, and storms bring heavy snowfall and strong winds that test the resilience of the lighthouse. Summers, by contrast, are pleasant, with average temperatures between 20 and 25 degrees Celsius, making it an ideal time for visitors to explore the area. The lighthouse's exposed position on the cliffs allows it to withstand powerful waves and gusts, making it a striking sight during both stormy and sunny weather when its white tower stands in stark contrast to the deep blue of the Atlantic.

Portland Head Light is one of Maine's most popular attractions, drawing thousands of visitors each year who are captivated by its scenic beauty and historical significance. The nearby Fort Williams Park provides ample space for picnics, walks, and exploration, with trails that lead to breathtaking viewpoints along the rocky coast. Visitors can also explore the lighthouse museum, housed in the former keeper's quarters, which displays artifacts, photographs, and stories detailing the lighthouse's history and the lives of the keepers who once tended to its light. The lighthouse has become a must-see for travelers to Maine, who are drawn by its timeless charm and the sense of peace that comes from standing at the edge of the ocean.

The area around Portland Head Light is characterized by rugged coastal vegetation, including wild grasses, beach roses, and juniper bushes that thrive in the salty, windswept environment. The nearby cliffs provide a habitat for seabirds such as herring gulls, cormorants, and eiders, which are frequently seen resting on the rocks or soaring over the waves. Harbor seals are also known to frequent the waters around Cape Elizabeth, delighting visitors with occasional sightings as they swim near the shore or bask on the rocks. The natural beauty of

LIGHTHOUSE: BEACON OF HISTORY AND LIGHT

the landscape, combined with the lighthouse's historical allure, makes Portland Head Light a treasured part of Maine's coastal ecosystem.

For the people of Cape Elizabeth and surrounding communities, Portland Head Light is more than a navigational aid; it is a symbol of local pride and a cherished landmark. Generations of Mainers have grown up with the lighthouse as a fixture in their lives, and it has become a source of inspiration for artists, photographers, and writers who seek to capture its timeless beauty. The lighthouse also serves as a reminder of Maine's rich maritime history and the resilience of coastal communities that have long depended on the sea. Each year, the Cape Elizabeth community celebrates its connection to the lighthouse through festivals, gatherings, and educational events, ensuring that the legacy of Portland Head Light continues to be passed down.

Maintaining Portland Head Light is no easy task, as the salty air, winter storms, and constant exposure to the elements take a toll on its structure. The tower requires regular maintenance to prevent erosion and damage, and periodic upgrades have been necessary to preserve its operational and historical integrity. Despite these challenges, the local community and preservation organizations have worked diligently to ensure that the lighthouse remains well-kept and accessible to the public. Through their efforts, Portland Head Light has been preserved as both a functioning lighthouse and a historical monument, showcasing the enduring significance of this coastal beacon.

One interesting fact about Portland Head Light is that it was the site of several shipwrecks in the 19th century, as even the powerful beam of the lighthouse could not always prevent accidents in the treacherous waters. The most famous incident occurred in 1898 when the schooner Annie C. Maguire ran aground on the rocks just below the lighthouse during a fierce storm. Miraculously, all crew members survived, and the incident added a layer of legend to the lighthouse's history. The event is still remembered today, with a plaque near the lighthouse commemorating the wreck of the Annie C. Maguire.

The significance of Portland Head Light extends beyond its function as a navigational aid. Situated along one of the busiest shipping routes on the East Coast, it has played a crucial role in supporting Maine's fishing and maritime industries by ensuring safe passage for vessels entering Portland Harbor. The lighthouse's light has guided countless ships through fog, rain, and darkness, protecting lives and cargo and reinforcing Portland's status as an important port. Its contribution to maritime safety has made it an invaluable asset, not just for Maine but for the entire New England region.

Portland Head Light is easily accessible by road, and its proximity to Portland makes it a popular day trip for both locals and tourists. The nearby Portland International Jetport connects the area to major cities across the United States, while Amtrak and bus services offer additional transportation options. Many visitors choose to drive along the scenic coastal routes to reach the lighthouse, enjoying the picturesque views of Maine's coastline along the way. Fort Williams Park, where the lighthouse is located, provides ample parking and amenities, allowing visitors to fully enjoy the experience of exploring the lighthouse and its surroundings.

Today, Portland Head Light stands as a beacon of history, beauty, and resilience. Its light continues to shine over the Atlantic, guiding ships and inspiring those who visit its shores. For locals and visitors alike, the lighthouse offers a chance to connect with the past, appreciate the rugged beauty of the Maine coast, and experience the tranquility that comes from standing on the edge of the ocean. Portland Head Light is not merely a navigational aid; it is a symbol of Maine's coastal heritage, a beloved landmark that will continue to illuminate the waters of the Atlantic for generations to come.

43. Punta Carretas Lighthouse - Uruguay

Punta Carretas Lighthouse, located at the southern tip of Montevideo, Uruguay, stands as a beacon of history and maritime guidance on the shores of the Rio de la Plata. Established in 1876, this modest yet striking lighthouse is a white cylindrical tower topped with a bright red lantern room, reaching a height of 21 meters. Its strategic position on the rocky coastline of Punta Carretas makes it an essential guide for vessels navigating the waters near Montevideo, particularly as they approach the bustling port of Uruguay's capital city. With its simple, classic design, Punta Carretas Lighthouse has become an emblem of Montevideo, drawing visitors and locals alike who come to admire its beauty and historical significance.

The history of Punta Carretas Lighthouse is intertwined with the growth of Montevideo as a major port city in South America. In the late 19th century, as Uruguay's economy began to expand, there was a growing need to protect ships navigating the tricky waters near Punta Carretas, where underwater rocks and sandbars posed a significant threat. The lighthouse was built to address these hazards, offering a steady light that could guide ships safely past the headland and into the nearby port. Over the decades, the lighthouse has seen various upgrades, transitioning from an oil lamp to a modern electric light, while preserving its classic architectural style and historic charm.

Punta Carretas experiences a temperate climate, with warm summers and mild winters typical of the region. Summer temperatures range from 25 to 30 degrees Celsius, while winters are cooler, averaging around 10 to 15 degrees Celsius. The lighthouse's coastal location exposes it to frequent winds, and the area often experiences high humidity, particularly in the summer months. Despite these conditions, Punta Carretas Lighthouse has remained resilient, standing tall against the occasional storms that blow across the Rio de la Plata, its light cutting through fog and mist to guide ships safely along Uruguay's coast.

Today, Punta Carretas Lighthouse is one of Montevideo's most cherished landmarks, attracting visitors who are drawn to its historical significance and scenic location. The surrounding area offers beautiful views of the Rio de la Plata and Montevideo's coastline, and the lighthouse itself provides a glimpse into Uruguay's maritime past. From its elevated position, visitors can enjoy panoramic vistas, watching as boats and ships make their way across the calm waters of the estuary. The lighthouse has become a favorite spot for photographers, who capture its iconic red-and-white silhouette against the blue skies and waters of Montevideo.

The rocky terrain around Punta Carretas Lighthouse is home to various coastal plant species, including hardy grasses, small shrubs, and wildflowers that thrive in the salty, windswept environment. The Rio de la Plata estuary supports a range of marine life, and seabirds such as gulls, terns, and cormorants are frequently seen near the lighthouse, taking advantage of the abundant fish in the waters below. The lighthouse's location also provides a peaceful escape from the urban hustle of Montevideo, as visitors enjoy the natural surroundings,

LIGHTHOUSE: BEACON OF HISTORY AND LIGHT

feeling the refreshing breeze and listening to the gentle waves lapping against the rocks.

For the people of Montevideo, Punta Carretas Lighthouse holds a special place in their hearts. It represents a connection to the city's maritime heritage and stands as a reminder of Uruguay's historical ties to the sea. The lighthouse has witnessed the development of Montevideo from a quiet port town to a vibrant capital, and it has become an enduring symbol of the city's identity. Locals often visit the lighthouse for leisure, enjoying its tranquil setting and reflecting on the legacy of their coastal community. The lighthouse has become a gathering place, where families, couples, and individuals come to watch the sunset over the estuary, appreciating the timeless beauty of Punta Carretas.

Maintaining Punta Carretas Lighthouse presents challenges, as the salty air, high humidity, and occasional storms accelerate wear on the structure. Regular maintenance is essential to preserve its historical and operational integrity, ensuring it continues to serve as a reliable navigational aid. The local authorities and preservation organizations have taken measures to protect the lighthouse, recognizing its cultural and historical importance. Restoration efforts have focused on reinforcing the structure, repainting the tower, and upgrading its lighting technology, while carefully preserving the original architecture that makes it such a distinctive part of Montevideo's skyline.

An interesting fact about Punta Carretas Lighthouse is that it was originally painted in alternating black and white stripes to make it more visible during the day. However, over time, the lighthouse was repainted in its current all-white design with a red lantern room, which has since become its signature look. Another lesser-known detail is that the lighthouse has played a role in Uruguay's military history, as its strategic location allowed it to serve as a lookout point during times of conflict. Today, the lighthouse stands as a peaceful monument, a testament to its resilience and adaptability through changing times.

The importance of Punta Carretas Lighthouse extends beyond its role as a navigational aid. Located along a major maritime route, it has provided essential guidance to vessels traveling between South America and Europe, as well as to ships entering the port of Montevideo. The lighthouse has contributed to Uruguay's economic growth by supporting the safe passage of goods and resources and fostering trade and commerce along the Atlantic coast. Its light has guided countless ships, offering safety and stability in the often unpredictable waters of the Rio de la Plata.

Montevideo is well-connected by various transportation options, making Punta Carretas Lighthouse accessible to both locals and international visitors. Carrasco International Airport, located just outside Montevideo, provides flights to major cities in South America and beyond, while the port of Montevideo serves as a hub for regional and international shipping. Public transport and taxi services make it easy for visitors to reach the lighthouse from anywhere in the city, and the area surrounding Punta Carretas offers a range of attractions, including shopping centers, restaurants, and parks, allowing visitors to explore the neighborhood before or after visiting the lighthouse.

Today, Punta Carretas Lighthouse stands as a beacon of history, beauty, and resilience. Its light continues to shine over the Rio de la Plata, guiding ships and inspiring those who visit its shores. For locals and tourists alike, the lighthouse offers a chance to connect with the past, to appreciate the rugged beauty of Uruguay's coast, and to experience the tranquility that comes from standing at the edge of the estuary. Punta Carretas Lighthouse is not merely a navigational aid; it is a symbol of Montevideo's coastal heritage, a beloved landmark that will continue to illuminate the waters of the Rio de la Plata for generations to come.

44. Ras Gharib Lighthouse - Egypt

Ras Gharib Lighthouse stands tall and resilient on the coast of the Red Sea, near the town of Ras Gharib in Egypt. Constructed in 1871, this lighthouse is one of the oldest on the Red Sea coast, a symbol of guidance and endurance in a region known for its harsh climate and rugged terrain. The lighthouse, with its distinctive black-and-white bands, reaches a height of 50 meters, towering above the surrounding desert landscape and marking the coastline for ships navigating the waters between the Suez Canal and the Red Sea. Its isolated, remote location along Egypt's eastern coast adds to its mystique and highlights its vital role as a beacon for maritime safety in this region.

The history of Ras Gharib Lighthouse is deeply connected to the expansion of global trade routes in the 19th century, particularly following the opening of the Suez Canal in 1869. The canal transformed maritime travel, connecting the Mediterranean and the Red Sea and reducing the journey between Europe and Asia. However, the Red Sea's coral reefs, shallow waters, and unpredictable currents posed significant challenges for vessels. The need for navigational aid to help guide ships safely through these treacherous waters led to the establishment of Ras Gharib Lighthouse. Built by French engineers, the lighthouse was constructed with a blend of functionality and durability to withstand the harsh desert conditions while serving as a reliable guide for seafarers.

The climate in Ras Gharib is arid and desert-like, with extremely hot summers and mild winters. Summer temperatures often exceed 40 degrees Celsius, while winter brings cooler weather, with temperatures ranging from 15 to 25 degrees Celsius. The Red Sea coast is known for its intense heat, high winds, and low humidity, conditions that pose unique challenges for the lighthouse's maintenance. Despite these extreme temperatures, the lighthouse's robust structure and its strategic design have enabled it to endure the elements, continuing to fulfill its purpose in one of the world's most challenging climates.

Though remote, Ras Gharib Lighthouse has become an intriguing destination for travelers, especially those with an interest in maritime history or the stark beauty of Egypt's coastal desert. Its towering silhouette against the bright blue skies and turquoise waters of the Red Sea offers a striking visual contrast, making it a fascinating subject for photographers and an emblem of resilience. Due to its isolated location, it is less frequented by tourists than other Egyptian landmarks, but this isolation only adds to its charm and the sense of solitude it offers visitors.

The area surrounding the lighthouse is characterized by sparse desert vegetation, such as hardy shrubs and salt-tolerant plants that can survive harsh conditions. The Red Sea itself is home to a vibrant marine ecosystem, renowned for its coral reefs and diverse sea life. The waters near Ras Gharib are frequented by seabirds like gulls, terns, and ospreys, which take advantage of the rich fishing grounds in the area. The contrast between the barren desert and the rich marine life in the Red Sea underscores the unique ecological balance of this region, where life thrives in unexpected places.

LIGHTHOUSE: BEACON OF HISTORY AND LIGHT

For the local community and the maritime industry, Ras Gharib Lighthouse holds significant importance. Its steady light, visible for miles across the water, serves as a trusted guide for fishermen, cargo vessels, and oil tankers traveling along the Red Sea coast. The nearby town of Ras Gharib has grown in part due to the oil industry, and the lighthouse has become a familiar landmark for the local workforce and residents, a reminder of the region's historical connection to the sea. The lighthouse's presence has created a sense of continuity, linking the town's modern-day economy with its maritime past.

Maintaining Ras Gharib Lighthouse is no easy feat. The high temperatures, sandstorms, and corrosive salt air contribute to the wear and tear on the structure, requiring regular upkeep to preserve its functionality. Additionally, its remote location poses logistical challenges, as maintenance crews must travel long distances to reach the lighthouse. Despite these challenges, the Egyptian government and local maritime authorities recognize the lighthouse's cultural and historical value, and efforts are made to ensure its preservation. Modern upgrades, such as the transition to solar-powered lighting, have been implemented to improve its efficiency while reducing the need for constant maintenance.

One interesting fact about Ras Gharib Lighthouse is its historical role in international navigation. In the late 19th century, it served as a vital marker along the Red Sea, a route used by ships traveling to India, East Africa, and beyond. The lighthouse's construction was part of a broader effort to create a network of lighthouses along the Red Sea, providing a lifeline for vessels in a region known for its challenging waters. Today, Ras Gharib stands as one of the few remaining operational lighthouses from that era, a testament to the enduring importance of traditional navigation aids in an age dominated by GPS technology.

The significance of Ras Gharib Lighthouse extends beyond its function as a navigational tool. Positioned along a major trade route, it has played a crucial role in supporting Egypt's maritime economy by ensuring safe passage for vessels transporting goods and resources. Its beam has guided countless ships, contributing to the safety and efficiency of trade along the Red Sea and reinforcing Egypt's strategic position as a gateway between the Mediterranean and the Indian Ocean. The lighthouse's historical and economic importance has cemented its status as a national landmark, representing Egypt's connection to the maritime world.

While Ras Gharib is remote, it is accessible by road from major Egyptian cities. The nearest major city is Hurghada, located about 150 kilometers to the south, which is a popular tourist destination and has an international airport connecting it to various countries. From Hurghada, visitors can reach Ras Gharib by car or local transport, following scenic desert roads that offer glimpses of the Red Sea coastline. For those interested in exploring the area, the journey to Ras Gharib Lighthouse provides a unique opportunity to experience the beauty and isolation of Egypt's coastal desert.

Today, Ras Gharib Lighthouse stands as a beacon of history, resilience, and beauty. Its light continues to shine over the Red Sea, guiding ships and inspiring those who visit its shores. For locals and travelers alike, the lighthouse offers a chance to connect with Egypt's maritime past, to appreciate the rugged beauty of the desert coast, and to experience the tranquility that comes from standing at the edge of the sea. Ras Gharib Lighthouse is more than just a navigational aid; it is a symbol of Egypt's enduring connection to the sea, a beloved landmark that will continue to illuminate the waters of the Red Sea for generations to come.

45. Reykjanesviti Lighthouse - Iceland

Reykjanesviti Lighthouse stands resiliently on the rugged Reykjanes Peninsula in Iceland, overlooking the vast and often turbulent North Atlantic Ocean. Built in 1908, this lighthouse is Iceland's oldest, and its white cylindrical tower topped with a red lantern room is a familiar and iconic sight against the wild, volcanic landscape of southwestern Iceland. At 31 meters tall, Reykjanesviti stands as a beacon of safety, guiding ships navigating these unpredictable waters and serving as a symbol of Iceland's enduring relationship with the sea.

The original Reykjanesviti Lighthouse, constructed in 1878, was damaged by an earthquake and had to be replaced with the current structure. Its construction took advantage of the local volcanic rock, blending practical architecture with the rugged Icelandic landscape. Perched on Bæjarfell Hill, the lighthouse was positioned to maximize visibility from the sea while withstanding the fierce North Atlantic winds. For over a century, it has provided a reliable light for sailors and fishermen, illuminating a coastline known for its treacherous waves, strong currents, and frequent storms.

The Reykjanes Peninsula, where the lighthouse is located, experiences a subpolar oceanic climate. Summers are cool, with temperatures ranging between 10 and 15 degrees Celsius, while winters are harsh, with temperatures hovering around freezing and high winds frequently battering the coast. Snow, rain, and fog are common, and the lighthouse often appears as a lone figure against dramatic Icelandic skies, shrouded in mist or silhouetted by storm clouds. Despite the challenging weather, Reykjanesviti Lighthouse remains a steadfast beacon, with its light penetrating the darkness, fog, and snowfall that frequently engulf the peninsula.

Reykjanesviti has become a popular destination for tourists, drawn by its remote beauty and the powerful landscapes of the Reykjanes Peninsula. The surrounding area is known for its geothermal activity, volcanic fields, and rugged coastline, making it a paradise for nature lovers and adventurers. Visitors to Reykjanesviti often marvel at the stark beauty of the volcanic rocks and cliffs, while the lighthouse itself has become a favorite subject for photographers, especially during the moody winter months when it stands against a backdrop of dark clouds and crashing waves. The area around the lighthouse provides breathtaking views of the ocean, and during clear weather, one can gaze out across the vast North Atlantic, feeling a profound sense of isolation and awe.

The flora and fauna around Reykjanesviti are unique to Iceland's subarctic environment. The landscape is mostly barren, with sparse vegetation consisting of hardy grasses, mosses, and small shrubs that cling to the rocky terrain. The surrounding waters, however, are rich in marine life, including seabirds such as puffins, kittiwakes, and guillemots that nest along the cliffs. During the summer months, visitors may spot seals lounging on the rocks or even catch a glimpse of whales and dolphins in the distance. This rugged environment, with its volcanic rocks and windswept cliffs, showcases the resilience of life in one of the world's harshest climates.

LIGHTHOUSE: BEACON OF HISTORY AND LIGHT

For the people of Iceland, Reykjanesviti Lighthouse is a symbol of their maritime heritage and a reminder of the island nation's reliance on the sea. The lighthouse has guided generations of Icelandic fishermen and sailors, offering them a sense of safety as they navigated the often dangerous waters surrounding their homeland. Reykjanesviti has become a cherished part of the Icelandic landscape, celebrated for its history, architecture, and enduring importance to the nation's maritime community. Today, it is more than just a lighthouse; it is a cultural landmark and a source of national pride, representing Iceland's connection to both its natural environment and its seafaring traditions. Maintaining Reykjanesviti is challenging, as the extreme weather conditions, salty sea air, and volcanic surroundings take a toll on its structure. The tower must be regularly inspected and repaired to ensure it withstands the elements, and the lighting system has been upgraded over the years to improve its efficiency and reduce maintenance needs. In recent decades, the lighthouse was modernized and automated, but careful preservation efforts have retained its original charm and historical integrity. Despite the challenges, the lighthouse remains in excellent condition, a testament to the dedication of those who have worked to preserve this essential piece of Icelandic heritage.

One interesting fact about Reykjanesviti Lighthouse is that its location on Bæjarfell Hill was chosen specifically to avoid the earthquakes that frequently occur in Iceland's volcanic zones. The original lighthouse, built closer to the shore, was damaged by seismic activity, leading to the decision to rebuild it on higher ground. This strategic location has allowed Reykjanesviti to endure the test of time, as it stands watch over a landscape shaped by fire and ice, enduring both the powerful forces of nature and the passage of centuries.

Reykjanesviti's importance extends beyond its role as a navigational aid. Positioned along a popular shipping route, it has played a crucial role in guiding vessels traveling between Europe and North America, contributing to the safety of international maritime trade. The lighthouse's light has served as a beacon of hope for sailors braving the North Atlantic, offering them a sense of security as they approach the Icelandic coast. As one of the oldest lighthouses in Iceland, Reykjanesviti is a vital part of the nation's infrastructure, supporting both local fishing communities and international vessels that rely on its guidance.

Reykjanesviti Lighthouse is accessible by road from Reykjavik, Iceland's capital, which is located about 50 kilometers to the northeast. The drive to the lighthouse offers stunning views of Iceland's volcanic landscapes, with black lava fields, geothermal hot springs, and rugged coastlines that create a surreal experience for travelers. The nearby Keflavik International Airport connects Iceland to major cities around the world, making Reykjanesviti a feasible destination for international tourists. Many visitors to Iceland's famous Blue Lagoon also take the opportunity to visit Reykjanesviti, as the two landmarks are located near each other on the Reykjanes Peninsula.

Today, Reykjanesviti Lighthouse stands as a beacon of history, resilience, and natural beauty. Its light continues to shine over the North Atlantic, guiding ships and inspiring those who visit its shores. For locals and tourists alike, the lighthouse offers a chance to connect with Iceland's maritime past, appreciate the raw beauty of the Icelandic landscape, and experience the awe-inspiring power of nature. Reykjanesviti is not merely a navigational aid; it is a symbol of Iceland's enduring spirit, a beloved landmark that will continue to illuminate the rugged coast of the Reykjanes Peninsula for generations to come.

46. Roter Sand Lighthouse - Germany

Roter Sand Lighthouse stands boldly in the North Sea, a distinctive red-and-white striped tower rising from the shallow waters near the mouth of the Weser River in Germany. Built between 1880 and 1885, this iconic lighthouse was a remarkable feat of engineering for its time, designed to guide ships safely through the treacherous sandbanks and strong currents off Germany's northern coast. Positioned over 30 kilometers from the nearest shore, Roter Sand is one of the first offshore lighthouses in the world and remains a symbol of resilience and innovation, enduring the harsh conditions of the North Sea for over a century.

The idea for Roter Sand Lighthouse emerged in the late 19th century, as maritime trade grew and the waters of the North Sea became busier with ships transporting goods to and from Germany's ports. The sandbanks near the Weser River mouth were a particular hazard, often causing ships to run aground. The German government recognized the need for navigational aid to mark these dangerous waters and commissioned the construction of Roter Sand Lighthouse. Its isolated location in open water required special planning and resources, and the construction faced several delays and challenges due to severe weather and logistical difficulties. However, by 1885, the lighthouse was completed and lit, standing as a beacon of safety for mariners.

Roter Sand Lighthouse is 30 meters tall, with a sturdy foundation that extends several meters below the seabed to withstand the North Sea's powerful waves and currents. The lighthouse's vibrant red-and-white stripes make it highly visible against the gray waters, and its light was once visible from a distance of 20 nautical miles. Though it has been decommissioned as a navigational aid, Roter Sand remains an iconic landmark, celebrated for its architectural design and historical significance. The tower's isolated position far from the land makes it an awe-inspiring sight, a lonely sentinel standing resolutely against the elements in the vast expanse of the sea.

The climate in this part of the North Sea is typically cold and windy, with frequent storms, especially in the winter months. Summers are mild, with temperatures rarely exceeding 20 degrees Celsius, while winters are often harsh, with strong winds, rain, and occasional snow. The lighthouse has been designed to endure these conditions, but the relentless saltwater and extreme weather take a toll on its structure, necessitating regular maintenance and repairs. Over the years, preservationists have made efforts to restore Roter Sand to its former glory, preserving it as a historical monument and a testament to German engineering.

Roter Sand has become a popular destination for maritime enthusiasts and adventurous travelers, drawn to its unique location and the story of its construction. While access to the lighthouse is limited due to its remote position, some organizations offer special tours, allowing visitors to experience the solitude and beauty of this offshore landmark. Standing on its deck, with the waves lapping against its base and the horizon stretching endlessly in all directions, visitors gain a sense of the vastness of the sea and the lighthouse's vital role in protecting those who once navigated these waters.

LIGHTHOUSE: BEACON OF HISTORY AND LIGHT

The marine environment around Roter Sand is home to a variety of wildlife. Seabirds such as gulls, cormorants, and gannets frequently circle the lighthouse, using it as a perch or resting point. The waters below are rich with fish, seals, and even porpoises, which thrive in the area's relatively undisturbed ecosystem. The North Sea's unique flora and fauna create a vibrant marine habitat, showcasing the resilience of life in an environment shaped by powerful tides and changing weather. The isolated nature of Roter Sand Lighthouse adds to the charm, as it stands surrounded by the raw beauty of the sea.

For the people of Germany, Roter Sand Lighthouse is more than just a navigational aid; it is a symbol of the nation's maritime heritage and engineering prowess. Built during a time of significant technological advancement, the lighthouse represents Germany's dedication to protecting its waters and ensuring the safety of its seafarers. The lighthouse has become an icon, featured in German literature, art, and even stamps, as a beloved part of the country's cultural landscape. Roter Sand's story continues to inspire admiration for the courage and skill of those who built and maintained it, as well as for the seafarers who relied on its guiding light.

Maintaining Roter Sand Lighthouse has always been a challenging task. The constant exposure to saltwater and storms has led to corrosion and wear on its structure, requiring frequent upkeep to prevent damage. Its remote location complicates repairs, as supplies and equipment must be transported by boat, and workers often contend with unpredictable weather conditions. Despite these challenges, preservation efforts have continued over the years, ensuring that the lighthouse remains intact as a historical monument. Today, Roter Sand is no longer in active service, but its light occasionally shines for commemorative events, honoring its legacy and role in maritime history.

One lesser-known fact about Roter Sand Lighthouse is its interior, which includes living quarters for the lighthouse keepers who once tended to it. These keepers faced long periods of isolation, as they were stationed in the lighthouse for weeks at a time, enduring the solitude and harsh conditions of the North Sea. The keepers' quarters, though small, were designed to be functional, providing them with a bed, kitchen, and even a small library. This aspect of the lighthouse's history adds a human element to its story, as one can imagine the dedication and resilience required to live and work in such a remote and challenging environment.

The significance of Roter Sand Lighthouse extends beyond its role as a navigational aid. Located on a busy maritime route, it has played a crucial part in supporting Germany's economy by ensuring the safe passage of ships transporting goods to and from the country's major ports. The lighthouse has helped prevent countless shipwrecks and accidents, contributing to the safety of maritime trade in the North Sea. Its importance to Germany's maritime infrastructure has earned it a place in the nation's history, celebrated as a symbol of safety and reliability in the often unpredictable waters of the North Sea.

Though located far from the mainland, Roter Sand Lighthouse is accessible by special boat tours from the German coast, particularly from the port of Bremerhaven. The lighthouse's isolation makes the journey an adventure in itself, with visitors traveling across the open sea to reach the iconic structure. The nearby port of Bremerhaven, a major hub of German maritime activity, serves as a gateway for both cargo and passenger ships, connecting Germany to international shipping routes. From here, vessels pass Roter Sand, recognizing its enduring role as a guardian of the North Sea's waters.

Today, Roter Sand Lighthouse stands as a beacon of history, engineering, and maritime heritage. Though its light no longer guides ships, its presence continues to inspire admiration and respect for the resilience of those who built it and the importance of protecting the seas. For visitors, Roter Sand offers a chance to connect with the past, to appreciate the beauty of the North Sea, and to experience the

LIGHTHOUSE: BEACON OF HISTORY AND LIGHT

tranquility of standing in a place that has seen the passage of time and tide. Roter Sand Lighthouse is not merely a structure; it is a symbol of Germany's connection to the sea, a beloved landmark that will continue to stand as a testament to human ingenuity and the enduring power of the ocean.

47. Sambro Island Lighthouse - Canada

Sambro Island Lighthouse, standing proudly off the coast of Nova Scotia, Canada, holds the distinguished title of being the oldest operational lighthouse in North America. Built in 1758, this historic lighthouse has been guiding mariners safely through the rocky waters of Halifax Harbour for over two centuries. Rising to a height of 24 meters, its tall white tower, accented with a red lantern room, makes it an iconic symbol of maritime heritage. Located on Sambro Island, roughly 6 kilometers from mainland Nova Scotia, the lighthouse occupies a rugged, isolated location that is both picturesque and crucial for navigation in the treacherous Atlantic waters.

The history of Sambro Island Lighthouse is rooted in the early days of British North America. After the establishment of Halifax in 1749, the port quickly became a strategic point for trade, defense, and maritime activity. However, the surrounding waters, dotted with rocks and shoals, posed a constant threat to ships. Recognizing the need for navigational aid, the British government authorized the construction of a lighthouse on Sambro Island in 1758, during the Seven Years' War.

LIGHTHOUSE: BEACON OF HISTORY AND LIGHT

The goal was to create a beacon that would guide ships into Halifax Harbour, contributing to the safety and success of the bustling port. Sambro Island's location in the North Atlantic subjects it to a maritime climate, characterized by cool summers and cold winters. Summer temperatures typically range from 15 to 20 degrees Celsius, while winter temperatures hover around freezing, with strong winds and storms battering the island. Fog is common in spring and fall, often shrouding the lighthouse in mist, adding a sense of mystery and isolation to its surroundings. The lighthouse's resilience in these conditions speaks to its sturdy construction, as it has weathered countless storms and hurricanes over the centuries, standing as a beacon of stability in a harsh environment.

Today, Sambro Island Lighthouse remains a beloved landmark and a point of pride for Nova Scotians. Although access to the island is limited due to its isolated location and lack of regular transportation, some tours allow visitors to experience the lighthouse up close. Those who make the journey are rewarded with spectacular views of the Atlantic Ocean, the rugged coastline, and the unique opportunity to stand beside a piece of history that has been part of Canada's maritime landscape for over 250 years. The lighthouse is frequently photographed and painted, its red and white structure contrasting beautifully with the deep blue of the ocean and the rocky shores.

The island's flora and fauna reflect its maritime setting. The rocky terrain is home to hardy coastal plants, including grasses, wildflowers, and salt-tolerant shrubs that cling to the thin soil. Seabirds such as gulls, cormorants, and eiders are a common sight, nesting along the cliffs and rocks around the lighthouse. The waters surrounding the island are rich in marine life, with seals often seen basking on the rocks and a variety of fish that attract larger marine mammals, including the occasional whale sighting. The island's natural beauty, combined with its historical significance, makes it a special place for both locals and visitors alike.

For the people of Halifax and Nova Scotia, Sambro Island Lighthouse is more than a navigational tool; it is a symbol of their maritime heritage and a cherished cultural landmark. Over generations, it has guided fishermen, traders, and travelers safely to shore, becoming a silent witness to the region's development and its close relationship with the sea. The lighthouse has played a role in countless lives, providing a sense of security and familiarity to those who work on the water. Its image has been featured in local art, literature, and tourism campaigns, solidifying its place in the hearts of Nova Scotians.

Maintaining Sambro Island Lighthouse is challenging due to its remote location and the relentless forces of nature. The salty air, strong winds, and frequent storms lead to corrosion and wear on the structure, necessitating regular upkeep to preserve its condition. Over the years, the lighthouse has undergone several restorations, with efforts focused on maintaining its historical integrity while ensuring it remains functional. Preservationists and local authorities have worked together to protect this national treasure, recognizing its importance to both the community and Canada's maritime history.

One fascinating detail about Sambro Island Lighthouse is its original lens, which was one of the first of its kind in North America. The Fresnel lens, a technological marvel at the time, allowed the lighthouse to cast a much stronger light than traditional lamps, reaching greater distances across the water. This advancement made Sambro Island a vital navigational aid in the region, significantly reducing shipwrecks and contributing to the safety of Halifax Harbour. The lens, now housed in a local museum, is a testament to the lighthouse's innovative beginnings and its contribution to the advancement of lighthouse technology in North America.

The significance of Sambro Island Lighthouse extends beyond its function as a guide for ships. Positioned along a major Atlantic trade route, it has played a crucial role in supporting the economy by ensuring safe passage for vessels entering and leaving Halifax Harbour.

LIGHTHOUSE: BEACON OF HISTORY AND LIGHT

The lighthouse has been instrumental in protecting lives and goods, making it an essential part of Canada's maritime infrastructure. Its light has been a steady, reassuring presence for countless mariners, a symbol of hope and safety in the often unforgiving waters of the North Atlantic.

The closest major city to Sambro Island Lighthouse is Halifax, which is well-connected by road, rail, and air. Halifax Stanfield International Airport provides flights to major cities in Canada and abroad, making it a convenient starting point for visitors interested in exploring Nova Scotia's coastal attractions. While regular transportation to Sambro Island itself is limited, private boat charters and seasonal tours provide access to the lighthouse, allowing adventurous travelers to experience its remote beauty and historical importance.

Today, Sambro Island Lighthouse stands as a beacon of history, resilience, and natural beauty. Its light continues to shine over the Atlantic, guiding ships and inspiring those who visit its shores. For locals and tourists alike, the lighthouse offers a chance to connect with Canada's maritime past, to appreciate the rugged beauty of the Nova Scotian coast, and to experience the tranquility that comes from standing at the edge of the ocean. Sambro Island Lighthouse is not merely a navigational aid; it is a symbol of Canada's enduring spirit, a beloved landmark that will continue to illuminate the waters of Halifax Harbour for generations to come.

48. Split Point Lighthouse - Australia

Split Point Lighthouse, standing proudly on a cliff along the iconic Great Ocean Road in Victoria, Australia, is a symbol of maritime heritage and natural beauty. Built in 1891, this striking lighthouse has guided countless vessels through the treacherous waters of Bass Strait. Towering at 34 meters, its white cylindrical tower with a bright red lantern room is a recognizable sight, contrasting beautifully against the green cliffs and blue ocean below. Known affectionately as the "White Queen," Split Point Lighthouse has become a popular destination, captivating visitors with its history, architecture, and the stunning landscapes that surround it.

In the late 19th century, as maritime traffic increased along Australia's southeastern coast, the need for a lighthouse at Split Point became apparent. The waters near Aireys Inlet, where the lighthouse stands, were notorious for hidden reefs and strong currents, and several shipwrecks had occurred in the area. The Victorian government commissioned the lighthouse's construction to enhance the safety of this vital route, guiding ships between Melbourne and other Australian ports. Designed with both practicality and elegance, Split Point

LIGHTHOUSE: BEACON OF HISTORY AND LIGHT

Lighthouse was completed in 1891, and its light was first lit on September 10 of that year. Over a century later, it remains an active beacon, ensuring the safety of those navigating the unpredictable waters.

The climate around Split Point is influenced by its coastal position, with mild summers and cool winters. In summer, temperatures range from 20 to 25 degrees Celsius, while winter brings cooler temperatures, averaging between 10 and 15 degrees. The area experiences frequent winds, and fog occasionally blankets the coastline, creating an atmospheric scene that only enhances the lighthouse's mysterious charm. The rugged landscape, shaped by winds and waves, is a testament to the lighthouse's resilience, standing firm against the elements in a region where the weather can change swiftly and dramatically.

Split Point Lighthouse has become a beloved landmark along the Great Ocean Road, drawing thousands of visitors each year who are eager to explore its history and enjoy the scenic views it offers. The lighthouse can be accessed by a short walk from Aireys Inlet, and visitors can climb to the top to experience panoramic views of the coastline and ocean. The sight of the ocean stretching out endlessly from the cliff is breathtaking, and for many, the lighthouse provides a sense of connection to Australia's maritime past. Split Point is a favorite spot for photographers and nature enthusiasts, and its iconic appearance has made it a popular setting in Australian media, further cementing its place in the cultural landscape.

The area around Split Point is rich in coastal flora and fauna, with native plants such as coastal wattle, saltbush, and wildflowers thriving along the cliff edges. The grasslands and heathlands surrounding the lighthouse provide a habitat for a variety of bird species, including sea eagles, hawks, and cormorants, which are often seen circling above. The waters below are home to seals, dolphins, and, during certain times of the year, migrating whales that add to the area's allure. The lighthouse, surrounded by such abundant wildlife, sits as a guardian over both land and sea, a silent witness to the natural rhythms of the coastline.

For the local community and visitors, Split Point Lighthouse holds deep significance. It represents a connection to Aireys Inlet's history and heritage, a reminder of the area's maritime roots. The lighthouse has guided generations of fishermen and sailors, its light a reassuring presence against the vast expanse of Bass Strait. The lighthouse has become a gathering point, where locals and travelers alike come to reflect on the power of nature and the courage of those who worked on and depended on the sea. Split Point has played an essential role in local culture, celebrated in stories, art, and community events that honor its legacy.

Maintaining Split Point Lighthouse presents challenges, as the salty air, high winds, and coastal climate contribute to wear on the structure. The white paint, which makes the lighthouse so striking, requires regular upkeep to prevent discoloration from the elements. Additionally, the steep cliffs and remote location complicate access for maintenance crews, adding to the difficulty of preservation. Despite these challenges, the lighthouse has been carefully maintained, with restoration efforts ensuring that it remains a safe and functional navigational aid. The community and government have both worked to preserve the lighthouse, recognizing its importance as a historical and cultural asset.

One interesting detail about Split Point Lighthouse is its original lens, which was a fixed light that had limited reach. In 1919, the light was upgraded to a rotating beacon, significantly enhancing its visibility. This upgrade allowed the light to be seen from a distance of 32 kilometers, making it a more effective guide for ships navigating the treacherous waters of Bass Strait. This lens, a Fresnel design, was a technological marvel of its time, and its introduction marked a new era for the lighthouse, increasing its safety and reliability.

LIGHTHOUSE: BEACON OF HISTORY AND LIGHT

Split Point Lighthouse's role as a navigational aid is vital for maritime safety. Positioned along a busy route, it has helped countless vessels navigate through Bass Strait, a notoriously challenging stretch of water. The lighthouse's light serves as a warning of the rocky reefs that lie hidden beneath the waves, a constant threat to ships traveling the Australian coast. Its contribution to maritime safety has earned it a place of honor among Australia's lighthouses, recognized for its dedication to protecting lives and cargo along one of the nation's key trade routes.

Split Point is easily accessible from Melbourne, making it a popular day trip destination for both locals and international tourists. The Great Ocean Road, one of Australia's most scenic drives, passes near the lighthouse, offering travelers a chance to explore the breathtaking coastal landscapes of Victoria. Regular public transport and tours from Melbourne provide convenient options for visitors, and many choose to continue their journey along the Great Ocean Road, discovering the region's natural beauty, historic towns, and vibrant communities.

Today, Split Point Lighthouse stands as a beacon of history, beauty, and resilience. Its light continues to shine over the Bass Strait, guiding ships and inspiring those who visit its shores. For locals and tourists alike, the lighthouse offers a chance to connect with Australia's maritime past, appreciate the raw beauty of the Victorian coast, and experience the tranquility that comes from standing at the edge of the ocean. Split Point Lighthouse is not merely a navigational aid; it is a symbol of Australia's enduring connection to the sea, a beloved landmark that will continue to illuminate the waters of the Great Ocean Road for generations to come.

49. St. Augustine Lighthouse - USA

St. Augustine Lighthouse, with its iconic black-and-white spiral design and bright red lantern room, stands proudly along the coast of St. Augustine, Florida, a beacon that has guided mariners through the treacherous waters of the Atlantic for over a century. Rising 50 meters (165 feet) above sea level, this lighthouse is both a symbol of maritime safety and a treasured historical landmark, its striking appearance instantly recognizable to locals and visitors alike. Situated on Anastasia Island, the lighthouse overlooks the Atlantic Ocean and the inlet that leads into Matanzas Bay, a location of both historical and navigational significance.

The history of the St. Augustine Lighthouse traces back to the 16th century when the first Spanish settlers arrived in Florida. A wooden watchtower initially marked the site, signaling the importance of the inlet as a route for explorers and traders. However, it wasn't until 1824, after Florida became part of the United States, that the first lighthouse was constructed on the island to properly serve the needs of increasing maritime traffic. This first lighthouse eventually fell into the ocean due to erosion, leading to the construction of the current lighthouse in

LIGHTHOUSE: BEACON OF HISTORY AND LIGHT

1874. The St. Augustine Lighthouse that stands today was built with remarkable precision and care, designed to withstand the relentless forces of nature and the passage of time.

Anastasia Island enjoys a humid subtropical climate, characterized by warm summers and mild winters. Summer temperatures often exceed 30 degrees Celsius, with frequent afternoon thunderstorms adding to the atmosphere of the coast. Winters are generally mild, averaging around 15 to 20 degrees Celsius, making the area a year-round destination for tourists. The proximity to the ocean brings a constant sea breeze, cooling the lighthouse and its surroundings during the hottest months. However, the region is also vulnerable to hurricanes, which have tested the lighthouse's resilience over the years. Despite facing powerful winds and storms, St. Augustine Lighthouse has endured, its design standing the test of time.

Today, St. Augustine Lighthouse is a popular tourist destination, welcoming hundreds of thousands of visitors each year who come to learn about its history, enjoy the scenic views, and perhaps even experience a touch of the supernatural, as the lighthouse is reputed to be haunted. Visitors can climb the 219 steps to the top, where they are rewarded with breathtaking views of the ocean, the city of St. Augustine, and the surrounding marshlands. The lighthouse has become a favorite subject for photographers and artists, its spiraled design and vibrant colors offering a striking contrast against the blue sky and green landscape of Anastasia Island.

The area around the lighthouse is home to a diverse ecosystem, including salt marshes, coastal hammocks, and a variety of plant and animal species adapted to the coastal environment. Trees such as live oaks and sabal palms provide shade and shelter for local wildlife, while marsh grasses thrive in the salty soil near the inlet. The waters surrounding Anastasia Island are rich in marine life, and dolphins are frequently spotted in the bay, delighting visitors with their playful antics. Seabirds like pelicans, seagulls, and ospreys are a common sight around the lighthouse, adding to the natural beauty of the area and underscoring the importance of the lighthouse in an environment where water and land coexist.

For the people of St. Augustine, the lighthouse is more than just a navigational tool; it is a cherished symbol of the city's heritage and a connection to its maritime past. The lighthouse has witnessed the evolution of St. Augustine from a small colonial settlement to a vibrant, thriving city. Over generations, it has stood as a silent guardian, watching over the sailors and fishermen who depended on its light to safely navigate the waters. Its presence has created a sense of continuity and identity for the community, and local residents take great pride in preserving the lighthouse and sharing its history with others.

Maintaining St. Augustine Lighthouse is no small feat. The coastal climate, with its high humidity, salt air, and frequent storms, accelerates the wear on its structure, necessitating regular upkeep to preserve its condition. The lighthouse's red lantern room, in particular, requires careful maintenance to prevent rust and fading caused by the salt air and intense sunlight. Restoration efforts over the years have been funded by local organizations and community support, reflecting the dedication of those who value the lighthouse as both a functional and cultural landmark. Today, the lighthouse is operated as part of the St. Augustine Lighthouse & Maritime Museum, which oversees its preservation and educational programs.

One fascinating fact about St. Augustine Lighthouse is its reputation for being haunted, with numerous reports of ghostly encounters and paranormal activity. Legend has it that the lighthouse is inhabited by the spirits of past keepers and the children of a worker who died during its construction. The stories have become an integral part of the lighthouse's allure, attracting curious visitors and paranormal investigators. The lighthouse has been featured in numerous television programs and documentaries, adding a layer of mystery and intrigue to its already rich history.

LIGHTHOUSE: BEACON OF HISTORY AND LIGHT

The importance of St. Augustine Lighthouse extends beyond its historical significance. Located along a busy shipping route, it has played a crucial role in ensuring the safety of vessels traveling along Florida's coast, helping to guide ships through the narrow inlet into Matanzas Bay. The lighthouse's beam, visible from over 20 miles away, has been a beacon of hope for countless mariners, its light cutting through fog and darkness to guide them safely to shore. Its contribution to maritime safety has been invaluable, particularly in a region known for its complex waterways and unpredictable weather.

St. Augustine is easily accessible by road, with the nearest major airport located in Jacksonville, about 50 miles to the north. The city is a popular tourist destination, known for its historical landmarks, beautiful beaches, and charming old-town atmosphere. Public transportation, along with local tours, provides convenient access to the lighthouse, making it a must-visit stop for those exploring St. Augustine. The lighthouse's position near popular beaches and parks also makes it a central point for exploring the natural beauty of Anastasia Island and the surrounding area.

Today, St. Augustine Lighthouse stands as a beacon of history, beauty, and resilience. Its light continues to shine over the Atlantic, guiding ships and inspiring those who visit its shores. For locals and tourists alike, the lighthouse offers a chance to connect with America's maritime past, to appreciate the rugged beauty of Florida's coast, and to experience the tranquility that comes from standing at the edge of the ocean. St. Augustine Lighthouse is not merely a navigational aid; it is a symbol of resilience and heritage, a beloved landmark that will continue to illuminate the waters of Florida for generations to come.

50. Tower of Hercules - Spain

The Tower of Hercules, standing on the coast of Galicia in northwestern Spain, is a monument of ancient ingenuity and endurance. Built by the Romans in the 2nd century AD, it is the world's oldest functioning lighthouse and the only Roman lighthouse still in use today. Rising 55 meters (180 feet) on a headland near the city of A Coruña, the tower has guided countless sailors across the centuries, serving as a beacon of safety and a remarkable relic of history. Its stone structure, meticulously crafted and maintained, has stood the test of time, weathering storms, wars, and changes in technology, remaining an enduring symbol of Spain's maritime heritage.

The Tower of Hercules was originally constructed by the Romans under the rule of Emperor Trajan, who sought navigational aid for ships approaching the rocky, fog-prone shores of Galicia. This region, known as "the end of the world" in ancient times, was notorious for its treacherous coastline and strong Atlantic currents. The lighthouse's Roman name, "Farum Brigantium," reflects its function as a faro or lighthouse, guiding mariners safely through the waters near the Galician coast. The original Roman structure stood at about 34 meters

LIGHTHOUSE: BEACON OF HISTORY AND LIGHT

(111 feet), with a ramp and internal spiral staircase—a remarkable feat of engineering that has survived nearly two millennia.

A Coruña enjoys a temperate oceanic climate, with mild winters averaging around 12°C (54°F) and warm summers reaching up to 24°C (75°F). The Atlantic's influence brings frequent rainfall, particularly in autumn and winter, and occasional coastal fog, adding to the mystique surrounding the tower. The lighthouse's elevated position on the headland makes it visible from miles away, its ancient silhouette often shrouded in mist. This combination of coastal weather and rugged landscape has enhanced the Tower of Hercules's reputation as a mysterious and timeless landmark.

Today, the Tower of Hercules is one of the most popular attractions in Galicia, drawing visitors from around the world who come to experience its history and the breathtaking views from its observation platform. Climbing to the top of the tower involves ascending over 200 steps, a journey that reveals the stonework and design techniques of the Romans. At the summit, visitors are rewarded with panoramic views of the Atlantic Ocean, the Galician coastline, and the city of A Coruña. Declared a UNESCO World Heritage Site in 2009, the tower is celebrated not only for its historical significance but also for its role in preserving Roman architecture and maritime culture.

The headland surrounding the Tower of Hercules is a designated parkland, covered in green grass, wildflowers, and low coastal vegetation adapted to the salty air and windy conditions. The rocky shoreline and cliffs provide habitat for seabirds, including gulls and cormorants, which are often seen nesting along the cliffs or flying over the waves. The coastal waters are home to a variety of marine life, including fish, seals, and occasionally dolphins, enhancing the natural allure of the lighthouse's surroundings. The site's flora and fauna add a touch of life and color to the otherwise imposing ancient structure, creating a unique blend of history and nature.

The Tower of Hercules holds a special place in the hearts of Spaniards, particularly the people of Galicia. It represents not only a connection to Spain's Roman past but also a symbol of resilience and cultural pride. Legends surrounding the tower include tales of Hercules himself, who, according to local myth, defeated a giant and buried his head on the site where the lighthouse was built. This tale has been passed down through generations, blending myth and history into the story of the tower, giving it a place in both Galician folklore and the Roman legacy. Due to its age and location, maintaining the Tower of Hercules has always posed unique challenges. The tower's original Roman core is remarkably intact, but later renovations and expansions, including a significant restoration in the late 18th century, have been necessary to preserve its structure. The coastal climate, with its salt-laden air and occasional storms, contributes to the gradual erosion of the stonework, requiring careful preservation efforts. Spanish heritage organizations oversee its maintenance, balancing the need to protect its ancient architecture with the demands of modern tourism.

One fascinating fact about the Tower of Hercules is that it is believed to be modeled after the Lighthouse of Alexandria, one of the Seven Wonders of the Ancient World. While the Alexandria lighthouse no longer stands, the Tower of Hercules carries on its legacy, providing a glimpse into the Roman approach to lighthouse design and engineering. Its interior ramp, used by Roman keepers to reach the light, is one of the earliest examples of such construction and remains a marvel of ancient architecture. This historical connection adds to the tower's significance, linking it to the broader heritage of ancient lighthouses.

The Tower of Hercules remains an essential navigational aid in the region, despite modern advancements in maritime technology. Its light, visible for nearly 20 nautical miles, serves as a critical guide for ships approaching A Coruña, where the Atlantic meets the coast of Spain. The tower's role as a beacon has evolved, from using wood fires to oil

LIGHTHOUSE: BEACON OF HISTORY AND LIGHT

lamps and now a modern electric light, but its purpose has remained the same—providing safe passage for vessels in one of Europe's oldest ports. In this way, the tower bridges ancient and contemporary seafaring traditions, a continuous thread through time.

Reaching the Tower of Hercules is easy for visitors, with A Coruña serving as a major travel hub in Galicia. The city is accessible by train, plane, and bus, connecting it with major Spanish cities like Madrid, Barcelona, and Santiago de Compostela. From A Coruña, local transportation, including taxis and buses, takes visitors directly to the site. The tower's accessibility has contributed to its popularity as a tourist attraction, allowing people from around the world to experience its grandeur and historical value.

As evening falls and the Tower of Hercules shines its light over the Atlantic, it stands as a monument to human achievement and endurance. For nearly two thousand years, it has weathered storms, witnessed history, and guided mariners safely through the waters. The Tower of Hercules is more than just an architectural marvel; it is a piece of living history, a symbol of Spain's heritage, and a testament to the resilience of ancient engineering. For those who visit, it offers a moment of awe and reflection, a place where history, myth, and the beauty of the sea converge.

51. Westerheversand Lighthouse – Germany

Westerheversand Lighthouse, located on the windswept marshlands of the North Sea coast in Germany, stands as an iconic symbol of resilience and maritime history. Built in 1906, this red-and-white striped lighthouse rises 40 meters above the ground, offering guidance to ships navigating the challenging waters off the coast of Schleswig-Holstein. Perched on a remote, grassy expanse surrounded by salt marshes and tidal channels, Westerheversand is one of Germany's most photographed lighthouses, its distinctive silhouette instantly recognizable against the vast, open landscape.

The decision to construct the Westerheversand Lighthouse was born out of necessity. In the early 20th century, the coastal waters around Schleswig-Holstein were perilous, with hidden sandbanks and strong currents posing constant threats to ships. A lighthouse was deemed essential to provide a beacon for vessels, guiding them safely through the unpredictable North Sea. Designed to endure the harsh coastal conditions, the lighthouse was constructed with reinforced materials,

LIGHTHOUSE: BEACON OF HISTORY AND LIGHT

and its bold red and white stripes made it easily visible against the marshy landscape. When it was lit in 1908, Westerheversand became a vital navigational aid, casting its beam far across the water.

The North Sea coast experiences a temperate maritime climate, with mild summers and cold, damp winters. The area is often blanketed by fog, particularly in spring and autumn, while the ever-present North Sea winds add to the lighthouse's isolation and mystique. Summers bring temperatures of around 15 to 20 degrees Celsius, while winter temperatures hover near freezing, with frequent rain and occasional snow. The lighthouse's remote location and exposure to the elements make it a testament to both human ingenuity and the power of nature. Westerheversand Lighthouse has withstood storms, high tides, and fierce winds, standing as a silent guardian over the marshes and coastline.

Today, Westerheversand Lighthouse is a beloved tourist destination, drawing visitors from around the world who are captivated by its beauty and historical significance. Accessible by a long walkway over the marshland, the lighthouse offers visitors a unique experience as they traverse the grassy plains to reach it. Once at the lighthouse, the view from the top is breathtaking, with panoramic sights of the North Sea, the tidal flats, and the serene, green marshes below. The lighthouse has become a favorite for photographers, capturing its silhouette against dramatic skies, and is frequently featured in German media as a symbol of the country's northern coast.

The salt marshes around Westerheversand are home to a rich variety of flora and fauna, adapted to the unique conditions of the coastal ecosystem. Hardy grasses, wildflowers, and salt-tolerant plants blanket the landscape, providing habitat for numerous bird species such as gulls, terns, and migratory birds that stop here on their journey across Europe. In the tidal flats nearby, one can often spot seals basking on sandbanks or swimming in the shallow waters. The area's biodiversity reflects the resilience of life in a challenging environment, adding a natural dimension to the lighthouse's cultural significance.

For the people of Schleswig-Holstein, Westerheversand Lighthouse is more than just a navigational aid; it is a cherished symbol of their heritage and connection to the sea. The lighthouse has guided fishermen, traders, and travelers safely to shore for over a century, becoming an integral part of the community's identity. It represents not only safety and guidance but also the strength and endurance of the coastal communities who have long depended on the sea for their livelihoods. Westerheversand's presence creates a sense of pride and continuity for locals, who see it as both a historical monument and a living part of their everyday landscape.

Maintaining Westerheversand Lighthouse presents unique challenges, as the salt-laden air, strong winds, and constant exposure to moisture contribute to the structure's wear and tear. The lighthouse requires regular upkeep to prevent corrosion and maintain its distinctive colors, which have become symbolic of the German coast. Despite these challenges, local authorities and preservationists have worked tirelessly to protect the lighthouse, recognizing its value as a historical and cultural asset. Modern restorations have carefully preserved its original design, ensuring that it remains a functional and iconic feature of the North Sea coast.

One interesting fact about Westerheversand Lighthouse is its dual role as both a navigational aid and a weather observation post. The lighthouse has historically been used to monitor weather patterns, tides, and sea levels, providing valuable data for understanding the North Sea's complex environmental conditions. Its isolated location and proximity to the open ocean make it an ideal site for gathering meteorological information, adding another layer to its significance. This dual role highlights the lighthouse's importance not only to maritime safety but also to environmental research and coastal management.

LIGHTHOUSE: BEACON OF HISTORY AND LIGHT

Westerheversand Lighthouse's contribution to maritime safety cannot be understated. Positioned along a busy shipping route, it has been instrumental in guiding vessels safely through the shallow waters and treacherous sandbanks that dot the North Sea coast. Its light has prevented countless shipwrecks, protecting lives and preserving cargo. The lighthouse's role in navigation has made it a cornerstone of Germany's maritime infrastructure, and its iconic image continues to remind people of the importance of lighthouses in ensuring safe passage for mariners.

Despite its remote location, Westerheversand is easily accessible from nearby towns. The nearest town, St. Peter-Ording, offers a range of accommodations and attractions, making it a convenient base for visitors exploring the region. The lighthouse is connected to the mainland by a raised footpath, allowing visitors to traverse the marshes without disturbing the fragile ecosystem. The path offers a scenic journey, with views of the grassy plains, tidal channels, and the open sea, setting the stage for the lighthouse's dramatic arrival. For those traveling by public transport, buses connect St. Peter-Ording with other parts of Schleswig-Holstein, while Hamburg, the nearest major city, provides further transport options to the region.

Today, Westerheversand Lighthouse stands as a beacon of history, natural beauty, and maritime heritage. Its light continues to shine over the North Sea, guiding ships and inspiring those who visit its shores. Westerheversand Lighthouse is not merely a navigational aid; it is a symbol of resilience, pride, and continuity, a beloved landmark that will continue to illuminate the waters of the North Sea for generations to come.

***

****

Milton Keynes UK
Ingram Content Group UK Ltd.
UKHW022018131124
451149UK00013B/1195